The
TEST VALLEY
TAPESTRY

The
TEST VALLEY
TAPESTRY

A unique work of art
depicting the history and
natural beauty of towns,
villages and parishes in the
Borough of Test Valley

Foreword by
Lord Denning

*Introduction and
tapestry descriptions by*
Cyril Pigott

First published 1995 by **Test Valley Borough Council**

© Test Valley Borough Council 1995
All rights reserved.

ISBN 0 952 6946 0 3

Maps reproduced from or based upon the Ordnance Survey Wessex Touring Map
and Guide with the permission of the Controller of Her Majesty's Stationery
Office. Crown copyright © All rights reserved.

Designed and typeset by BAS Printers in Adobe Janson and Monotype Gill Sans.

Printed by BAS Printers Ltd, Over Wallop, Stockbridge, Hampshire

ISBN 0 952 6946 1 1

CONTENTS

HAMLETS, VILLAGES, PARISHES AND TOWNS IN THE TAPESTRY

BOROUGH OF TEST VALLEY

This map shows the Test Valley Borough/Hampshire County boundary when the Tapestry was being worked. Later, in 1992, South Tidworth became part of Wiltshire.

The detailed descriptions of each Tapestry panel include a map of the local area depicted.

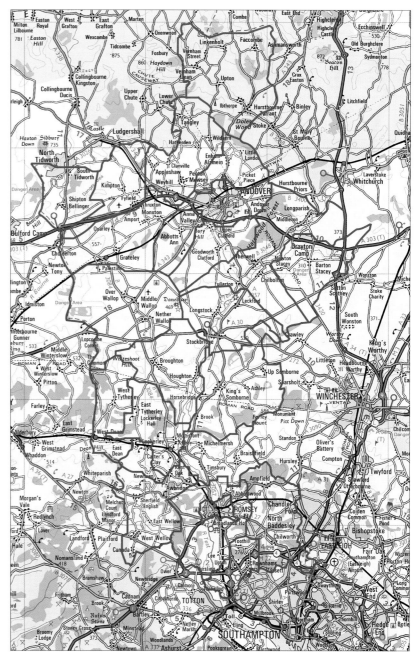

FOREWORD

In June 1990 Lord Denning, an illustrious former pupil of the Andover Grammar School, who lives near the River Test at Whitchurch, opened the first public exhibition of the 'Test Valley Tapestry' in the Andover Museum (formerly the Grammar School building).

FROM LORD DENNING

I wish to commend this book which tells the story of villages and towns in our lovely Test Valley. Good folk in each of these contributed to it.

Our villages in the Test Valley go back over 1,000 years to the days of Alfred the Great. The villagers built their cottages near the river so as to have access to water and to be available for their animals. They got their water from wells. They built churches of chalk and flint. They were a fine race.

The Tapestry is a splendid record of the past and I do hope many will see it and appreciate its beauty and the work that has gone towards the making of it.

It was Laurie Porter who conceived the project and did much towards its execution. It is sad that he did not live long enough to launch this book but he will be remembered as the mainspring of it. It is, in a way, a memorial to him.

Denning

PREFACE

The Borough of Test Valley, so beautifully depicted in the 'Test Valley Tapestry', is one of Hampshire's largest local authority areas covering some 245 square miles. Its population of 102,000 is spread almost equally between the two main towns (Andover and Romsey) and the hamlets and villages in the surrounding countryside.

The valley of the River Test, and its tributaries, forms the back bone of what is arguably one of the most attractive areas in England, rich in history and natural beauty. It is a delight to those who live here and those who visit.

Test Valley District Council came into being in April, 1974, with the amalgamation of the Boroughs of Andover and Romsey and the Rural Districts of Andover, Romsey and Stockbridge. Subsequently granted Borough Council status, Test Valley comprises 56 civil parishes almost all of which are represented in the 'Tapestry'.

The justifiable pride in which the Test Valley is held by the local community is amply demonstrated in the 'Tapestry', to which so many throughout the Borough have contributed.

Test Valley Borough owes a considerable debt of gratitude to all of these people. They would, I believe, be amongst the first to acknowledge that the project, which is a fine and unique example of community cooperation, would not have come about in the first place without the imagination and tenacity of former Andover and Test Valley Mayor, Laurie Porter.

I do hope that you will enjoy reading this book. In my view it encapsulates the character of the area, both pictorially and by revealing significant events not only of the last decade during which the 'Tapestry' was being made, but of past centuries, in a way that no other guide or reference book could achieve.

If you do not live locally the book may whet your appetite to come and find out more. Where better to start than by viewing the 'Test Valley Tapestry' here at Beech Hurst, in Andover?

Finally, I wish to record special appreciation to Cyril Pigott for his very thorough research in preparation for this book, and the introduction and detailed descriptions of each panel; to Robina Orchard for the section on the design and execution of the embroidery; to my Assistant Nigel Sacree for his enthusiasm in 'pulling the threads together' and to BAS Printers Ltd. for their active support and care in the production of the book.

Gerry Blythe

Chief Executive
Test Valley Borough Council

INTRODUCTION

The Test Valley 'Tapestry' was completed in 1994, ten years after the ambitious idea was initiated by the late Mr Laurie Porter.

While the 'Tapestry' is technically embroidery, alliteration and historical precedent prevail.

By any standard it is a remarkable and impressive example of community co-operation as well as a strikingly beautiful work of art, unique in this country. It will give succeeding generations pleasure and an historical perspective of the area and the age.

Laurie Porter

Laurie Porter was born and bred in Andover, growing to love the beautiful Test Valley. A schoolmaster, he taught at schools in Romsey and Andover and was actively involved in public life, serving twice as Mayor of Andover Borough and once as Mayor of Test Valley Borough.

It was during his year of office as Test Valley Mayor, from 1983 to 1984, that he first dreamed of capturing the Test Valley in wool and canvas. He perceived the finished work on the lines of the Bayeux Tapestry but in separate panels.

In a paper dated 9th February, 1984, he drew his fellow Councillor's attention particularly to the Bayeux Tapestry and suggested that the natural beauty and rich, varied history of the area should be portrayed in a similar manner. The paper invited discussion by Councillors on the 'feasibility of providing a Test Valley Mural Tapestry for the Guildhall Council Chamber, Andover'.

It was suggested that the project could 'be carried out by voluntary effort over a period of perhaps three or four years'. The whole tapestry would comprise ten panels each 42 inches wide and 24 inches high, three depicting the Andover area, three the Romsey Area and the remainder 'devoted to groups of wards'.

A centre strip of 18 inches 'could display a stylised panoramic representation of the urban and rural Test Valley scene', while a frieze 3 inches wide top and bottom could provide space for historical information not included in the main panel, examples of local industries, flora and fauna and aspects of modern life.

For technical and artistic support, guidance, and encouragement, Mr Porter was very pleased to be able to rely on the capable assistance of local embroiderers Robina Orchard and Meg McConnell.

An attempt was made to cost the project, the paper concluding: 'Over a period of perhaps four years the total cost of materials might therefore be between £500 and £600 allowing for contingencies. The "tapestry" when finished, comprising between three and four million stitches, would probably be valued for insurance at several thousand pounds.'

In a prophetic note Mr Porter wrote: 'The project would involve so much voluntary work over so long a period, that it is not worth doing unless the final result were to be the finest possible and of an artistic quality which could not be outdone by any other Borough in the Country.' Councillors were enjoined to enlist volunteers to implement the project.

Realising that he needed to canvass a wider audience he then sent copies of his paper to all the Parish Councils and the Women's Institutes in the area. His persistence fortunately paid off and gradually villages began to respond positively, submitting original sketches to him for vetting. Meanwhile, the Test Valley Borough Council had agreed to finance the cost of materials from its Lottery Fund.

No one could possibly have envisaged that the project would take ten years to come to fruition nor that the final result would be almost twice as large as Laurie Porter's original dream (far too large to be housed in the Andover Guildhall), with nearly every parish in the Borough being involved.

Sadly, he did not live to see the completion as parts of the last two panels were still being worked when he died in May 1993 at the age of 75. The Test Valley Tapestry will be his enduring memorial.

The Houghton, Bossington, Broughton panel being presented to Test Valley Borough Mayor Mrs. Pamela White.

Villages tackled the project in varying ways depending not only on the artistic talents available but also on who should be involved. In King's Somborne it was decided from the outset that anyone should be allowed to help, regardless of experience. The canvas with the design painted on it, went from one village organisation to another, from house to house and to the village school where every one of the 100 pupils contributed a few stitches under careful supervision. In the end about 320 individuals (whose names were recorded behind the panel) had a hand in its production. It was the first to be finished and was handed over in the Autumn of 1987.

At the other end of the scale some were designed and executed by an individual, or a select few. Unable to contemplate the formidable task of producing a whole panel (258,000 stitches!) most parishes worked a third or less, sharing the panel with adjacent villages.

Collectively, they encapsulate an abundance of wildlife and a pageant of history, together with important buildings and monuments, beauty spots, industries, local characters and contemporary events: an incredible visual time capsule.

As the project gathered momentum in the late eighties and more villages were encouraged to participate, Laurie realised that the original time scale for completion was quite unrealistic.

In 1990 he set an optimistic deadline asking for the work to be completed by the end of May of that year. In a ceremony at Cricklade Theatre, Andover, in June 1990, representatives of the tapestry groups handed over their panels to the then Mayor of Test Valley, Councillor Mrs Pamela White.

'This is now part of the history of Test Valley for ever and a day', she said as she warmly thanked Laurie Porter for his 'determination, tenacity and diplomacy in getting the project off the ground and keeping it on course'. Each parish received a full size photographic copy of its panel for permanent display locally.

In the following month the embroidered panels went on public display for the first time at Andover Museum in an exhibition opened by Lord Denning.

Later, they were displayed in Stockbridge Town Hall and Romsey Abbey, enabling 2,000 people to see them and marvel at their diversity and workmanship.

The publicity prompted the very few parishes not involved to start work without delay. Ultimately most parishes in the Borough, including some seventy hamlets and villages, and the towns of Andover and Romsey are represented. Laurie's original dream has been more than fulfilled.

Subsequently, advice having been sought from the Victoria and Albert Museum about framing, the panels were hung in the Conference Suite of the new Test Valley Borough headquarters building at Beech Hurst, Andover. Here, the irreplaceable and priceless tapestries are secure and in a suitably controlled environment and open for public inspection by appointment.

Lord and Lady Denning (right) at Andover Museum, with Laurie Porter and Cllr. Mrs. Pamela White

The Tapestry has spawned a number of projects, including a musical composition entitled the 'Test Valley Tapestry Suite', commissioned by Test Valley Borough Council, with the support of Southern Arts and the Hampshire County Council.

This suite, comprising eleven separate pieces of folk music, was composed by John Kirkpatrick. It was performed on classical and folk instruments in Andover and Romsey in May, 1992, by an ensemble comprising the composer and five other musicians including four members of the Bournemouth Sinfonietta.

Some of the melodies were subsequently adapted for performance by school musical groups. Roger Watson of the Traditional Arts Projects visited each of the seven primary schools associated with the Test Valley School, Stockbridge, working with children to compose suitable lyrics. Sandra Howlett worked with the music teachers in the schools teaching the songs to individual choirs: *Welcome Song* – Broughton; *The River* – Stockbridge; *The Farmer's Life* – Wherwell; *The World Keeps Turning Round* – Wallop; *The Ballad of Lockerley School* – Lockerley; *Grey and Green* – West Tytherley; and *The Tapestry* – Stockbridge.

Test Valley Tapestry Suite Composer John Kirkpatrick (accordion and concertina), Sue Harris (oboe and hammered dulcimer), Suzanne Kingham (violin), Jane Coster (flute), John Ewart (bassoon) and Andrew Baker (double bass)

In July 1993 the Suite, this time performed by a massed choir of children and seven instrumentalists of the Hampshire Music Service under the baton of Richard Howlett, delighted a huge audience at the Test Valley School, which included Mrs Glenys Porter, Laurie's widow.

The music has also been arranged for band performance by local musician Major Ron Berry.

In order to make the Tapestry as accessible as possible, the Borough Council produced full size laminated photographic copies, which have been in popular demand for exhibitions and talks. Full size copies are also displayed at the Council's Duttons Road, Romsey, offices. Awareness of the Tapestry further afield has been stimulated by articles in local and regional newspapers, national magazines and a BBC South Television broadcast. Colour postcards have been produced, which have gone all over the country and abroad.

No-one fortunate enough to be able to examine the Tapestry can fail to be impressed by the astonishing range, beauty and detail of this unique representation of the Test Valley. Everyone connected with it in any way should be intensely proud of their involvement with the project.

'IN THE BEGINNING'

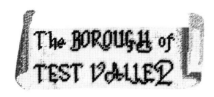

A personal overview of the initiation of the Tapestry, by Robina Orchard

I completed all my embroidery exams shortly before meeting Laurie Porter. He told me about his dream. We both had seen the Domesday exhibition and woodcarving of the Bayeux Tapestry in the Guildhall at Winchester and the idea of portraying the Test Valley in stitches was laid.

I had already used a scene from our village of Amport on one of my exam pieces, but this was not canvas work. The thought of helping with the Test Valley Tapestry was like a magnet. I introduced an embroidery teacher, Meg McConnell, to Laurie. Meg lived locally in the village of Monxton and we had met whilst taking the final part of our exams. Between us we helped Laurie at the launch and throughout the 'surgery' meetings held every few months at the Guildhall in Andover. It was at these meetings that all aspects of the work were discussed including stitches and size of canvas.

Meg and I gave suggestions about tackling design ideas for the main scenes. These were brought to subsequent meetings – ball point sketches on graph paper, beautiful pastel drawings or watercolour paintings by local artists. It was from the Houghton, Bossington and Broughton panel that I chose the colours. We agreed that the centre section should contain a limited selection of stitches whilst the borders should be kept simple using mainly Tent Stitch.

As the centre panels were being worked we decided to have a uniform colour within the borders of all the 'tapestries.'

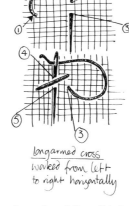

longarmed cross worked from left to right horizontally

Long Armed Cross Stitch

Also the borders should be enhanced by outlining with Long Armed Cross Stitch in blue at the top and green for the lower border with dividing lines in either colour where appropriate. There were no typed instructions so our information was adapted as it was transmitted from scribe to technician!

JOINING

The panels were joined by backstitch into every hole allowing a seam of about four rows. It was suggested that stitching should stop about half an inch from the seam. This allowed for turnings to be folded back and then stitched over to continue the picture. I worked the Monxton, Amport and Grateley panel this way. You will notice that it is quite difficult to detect the joins. Many of the other panels were either worked as a whole canvas or not designed to join as one scene. This problem was overcome by stitching over the join with Long Armed Cross Stitch.

EMBROIDERY STITCHES

These gradually crept in to enhance the scenes. We knew that this would work as the 'tapestries' were to be glazed and hung as pictures. Similar scenes could be used for cushions, stool covers or even communion kneelers, in which case the stitches should be firmly attached to the canvas avoiding loose embroidery stitches.

French Knots were used throughout the panels to depict sheep, flowers, blossom, and in my panel, centre section, as a cow parsley border between

French Knot

the village green and the road. Three colours were used together, yellow, green and white. On the same panel in the Grateley section the horse chestnut flowers were worked quite freely, as were the daffodils scattered throughout the Thruxton, Fyfield and Kimpton panel.

It is always difficult to portray detail in confined spaces and to create with accuracy. Many examples were tried on spare canvas before proceeding. In the Tangley, Hatherden and Wildhern panel the practice paid off as the sewers carefully outlined the tent-stitched cricketers in black stranded embroidery thread giving the players real movement.

Sheaf Filling Stitch was used for the Maypole dancers and for Mrs 'Mac's' fur coat in the Monxton, Amport and Grateley panel. The dresses were white trimmed with blue rick rack. The braids were whipped as was the iron fence of Grateley school.

CANVAS STITCHES

Even to the uninitiated these panels are full of ingenuity and imagination. I hope to highlight some of these interpretations by explaining the variety of stitches.

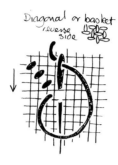

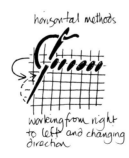

Tent Stitch

A number of panels have been worked predominantly in Tent Stitch. This gains nothing from light reflections – appearing completely flat like a woven surface. When this stitch is used, colour has been carefully selected to draw our eyes to specific features. This is one of the few stitches which could have given a real feeling of a painting if a little more highlighting had been included. It is a very time-consuming stitch and those sections which were worked by one individual will have taken many hours. The Abbotts Ann panel was worked this way by one person who also selected his own colours – a mammoth task.

Countryside

Fields adorn many panels, and it is their portrayal which particularly intrigues me. I admire the inventiveness shown here: cut and uncut corn, harvesters and tractors, ploughed fields and meadows, cattle and sheep. Perhaps there should have been a pig or two somewhere – there are lots around!

Some stitches represented are Encroaching Gobelin, Brick, Cross, Florentine, Cashmere, Diagonal and Long Armed Cross. The Clatfords and Barton Stacey panel includes an interesting combination of Chain and Brick Stitches.

Florentine Stitch

7

Bushes and Trees

These are worked in many types of stitch. The very effective Cross Stitch, sometimes interspersed with Tent Stitch, gives a little added texture. French Knots are popular, and sometimes are worked quite loosely. For distant trees Hungarian Stitch and an adaptation of Florentine Stitch work particularly well. They both travel quickly over the canvas and with a good blend of colour in the needle instantly depict the subject. However, if it's real detail you like then Leaf Stitch or Fan Stitch are used to their full advantage in a few panels.

Leaf Stitch used for the ear of corn on the Map.

Leaf Stitch

Water

The rivers and streams show very little variety of stitches. Florentine and Brick Stitch variations are the most popular and reflect the glistening ripples of the chalk streams which flow throughout the county. Silk threads have been used with wools to illustrate the jewel-like qualities in the rivers as they babble along.

Sheep

As you pass through this scenic area at certain times of the year sheep dominate the fields. These creatures are portrayed in amusing and devious ways. Some sheep are tidily stitched in Tent Stitch whilst others are shown in their rough dress of tousled wool. Needless to say the varieties of sheep are endless. Some have round faces and tight bubbly curls of wool, whilst others have ringlets and black noses and feet. The 'Test Valley Sheep' as I am sure they will be known seem to have developed their own particular characters.

Detailed tapestry section of sheep

Buildings

Chequered patterns of brick and flint can be seen in many of our villages. Longparish and Kimpton have fine examples. Once again these features have been ingeniously portrayed with blends of thread and imaginative directional stitching to catch the light. Stitches include Smyrna or Double Cross, Flat and Upright and Basic Cross.

Brick houses in this area seem to be generally modern or Victorian. Flint is still used on occasions for decorative purposes. Bricks are depicted using several stitches from Tent and Flat to Straight Gobelin, Hungarian and diagonal – all to excellent effect.

Thatched cottages abound in almost every village. Inventive stitches have been used to portray the rustic properties of the roofs. For the Penton panel Flat stitch was used effectively whilst others developed variations of Encroaching Gobelin Stitch. Stockbridge has used a version of Florentine Stitch for its new golden thatch by the river.

Snow

We do get snow now and again in the valley, although some villages are more exposed than others. Several of us managed to work the seasons into our panels in quite a subtle manner – by portraying spring bluebells with summer flowering roses, autumn blackberries and winter trees. Only one panel (Vernham Dean) shows a beautiful interpretation of snow clad thatches and fields blending into the other seasons. Icicles hang down from the roof in front of the tiny window in the centre of the picture. Rhodes Stitch with an interesting blend of colours is used for the snowy thatch.

Working from photographs and sketches on the Knights Enham, Enham Alamein panel

WORKING FROM PAPER TO CANVAS

Many of the Test Valley canvases were drawn using waterproof ink, sometimes using a photograph underneath the canvas. Outlined drawings on paper can be enlarged on photocopiers.

My experience is that working from a main coloured design and photographs is easier than painting the canvas with oils or acrylic paint. The painted method was used for the Amport section, which was thought to be easier for novices. However, this was not as straightforward as had been hoped.

Inspired by the Test Valley Tapestry, I subsequently worked on another much larger canvas picture. This hanging is bigger than a single bed, being 6ft x 4ft with only an 18in square area of detail worked in Tent Stitch. I used the fast moving Brick Stitch for the remainder. The original cartoon took all my efforts. Laying the canvas over the painting I marked the indicating lines with waterproof ink. The main feature's size was worked out on graph paper. (I mention this should you also feel compelled to put your ideas into stitches, having yourself been inspired by the Tapestry.)

Original colour design for a panel

THE MAP

In order to standardise the size of the Stockbridge panel we agreed that a map of the Borough of Test Valley should be added, so it was almost an afterthought. This had to be worked on 24 threads to the inch canvas. I used Appleton's crewel wool, with pearlé thread for the lettering, and stranded DMC embroidery threads for the coat of arms, compass and lower border lettering.

This was very time consuming, taking about an hour to complete a square inch. I adapted the lettering and experimented with threads of varying thicknesses. I had thought of working it like an old parchment in greys and sepia tones but the coloured one was preferred to blend with the colours of Stockbridge.

The sheep are being driven from Wales through Stockbridge to the Weyhill Fair made famous by Thomas Hardy. I worked from a photograph of the Test Valley Borough coat of arms. The extract from Tennyson's 'The Brook' was quoted by Lord Denning at the first public exhibition at Andover Museum in 1990.

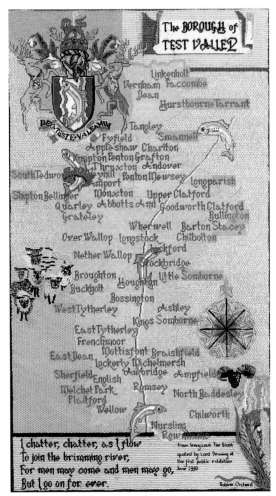

The Test Valley Borough map from the Stockbridge panel

The ram, poppy, ears of corn and compass with its engraved prisms, are all worked in surface stitches. The stitches employed are Byzantine Stitch and a woven Spider's Web for the poppy; Leaf Stitch for the corn; and Chain Stitch with a little Needle Weaving for the grasses.

The ram is in French Knots with Blanket Stitch horns.

You can see that the river rises north-east of Andover and flows out into Southampton Water. It passes through Lord Denning's area of Whitchurch just before entering into the Borough of Test Valley. Many tributaries join it on its journey through Stockbridge with its famous fishing club, indicated by the central trout.

TECHNICAL DETAIL

Appleton's Crewel wools were chosen to enable the stitcher to blend the colours. Short lengths are advised as the canvas wears the threads. Stranded embroidery threads can be used with the wool to give the luminescent effect on subjects like kingfishers, fleshy leaves, fish and rivers. Generally three threads were used in the needle for maximum cover of the canvas. However, this was not a hard rule as some types of stitches required less thread.

SPECIFICATIONS

Canvas	16 threads per inch – worked in frames
Panel Size	Overall 24in x 42in (the width of the finished panels actually varies from 42in to 45in)
Borders	(top and bottom) 3in
Middle Section	18in
Border Frame	Long Armed Cross
Other Stitches	Tent/Half Cross and many canvas stitches including embroidery surface stitches.
Thread	Appletons Crewel wool and stranded embroidery threads.

There were variations on the 'standard' specification, for example, the Test Valley map was worked at 24 threads to the inch: the Abbotts Ann panel has top and bottom borders 4 inches deep, the middle section measures 16 inches; the overall width of the panel is 36 inches and it was worked at 18 threads to the inch.

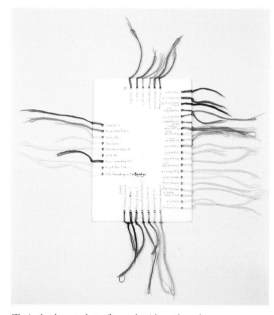

Typical colour palette for embroidery threads

THE TAPESTRY PANELS

Vernham Dean
Linkenholt
Upton
Faccombe
Hurstbourne Tarrant

VERNHAM DEAN, LINKENHOLT, UPTON, FACCOMBE and HURSTBOURNE TARRANT

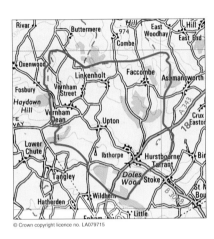

© Crown copyright licence no. LA079715

These villages comprise the United Benefice of Hurstbourne Tarrant (St Peter), Faccombe (St Barnabas), Vernham Dean (St Mary the Virgin) and Linkenholt (St Peter). Faccombe is not only the most northerly parish in Test Valley Borough but, at 800 feet above sea level, the highest, commanding wonderful views over the North Wessex Downs into Wiltshire and Berkshire. Its neighbour, Linkenholt, a tiny, remote community little more than a collection of farm buildings, is also rich in scenic beauty. From here the ground falls steeply into Vernham Dean, a parish which embraces several hamlets including Upton. It is here that the Bourne Rivulet has its source although it is the River Swift that flows through Upton to join the Bourne at Hurstbourne Tarrant. Clustered round the pond in the centre of the village are a number of picturesque thatched cottages. Three counties – Hampshire, Wiltshire and Berkshire – meet in this corner of the Test Valley.

Hurstbourne Tarrant was a Saxon settlement (Hissaburnham), part of the extensive King's Forest. In 1266 Hurstbourne was granted to the Cistercian nunnery at Tarrant in Dorset, hence the name. Writer William Cobbett loved the village, staying often with his friend Joseph Blount at Rookery Farm where he wrote much of his 'Rural Rides'. He made more than 20 references to 'the village of Uphusband, the legal name of which is Hurstbourne Tarrant'. In one he commented 'I love this place'. The very large gravestone of his friend Joseph is just inside the lych gate of the church. He left instructions that the stone should be large enough for children to play marbles on.

Top border

Badge of the Women's Institute and the Hampshire Rose; the *emblem of the Game Conservancy*, of which the Faccombe Estate, now some 4,000 acres, is part; *ghost of a cleric* haunting Conholt Hill. Legend has it that during the plague of 1665, the Rector, terrified of catching it, persuaded the victims to assemble on the top of the hill, promising to take them food and medicine. Instead, he abandoned them. But he eventually contracted the disease and succumbed. Many have claimed to see his ghost; the *sign of Manor Farm Dairy*; the *flag of Linkenholt Cricket Club*; the *special stamp to commemorate the engagement of Prince Andrew and Miss Sarah Ferguson*. The *crest of the Mothers' Union*; the *sign of the Boot Inn*, now a private house; the *badge of the Royal British Legion*; *Riding for*

the Disabled; *Halleys Comet* which appeared
in 1986. The comet is also featured in the
Bayeux Tapestry. The *badge of the Girl Guide
movement*; the *Olympic Games rings* marking
the 1988 games in Seoul.

Middle section

The four churches naturally figure
prominently. At the top, towards the left,
below the cricket club flag, is *St Peter's,
Linkenholt*. This was moved from behind
the Manor in 1871. Parts of the old church,
including the 12th century south doorway,
were retained. The drum-shaped font with
tapering sides is Norman. Opposite, on the
right is *St Barnabas, Faccombe*. This was built
in 1866 of stone and flint in 14th century
style. It replaced the smaller church of
St Michael in the hamlet of Netherton. The
font and some of the memorial tablets were
transferred to the new church. The scenery
between the two churches represents the
view from Vernham Dean church looking
up to Linkenholt. *St Mary's, Vernham Dean*
is seen below Linkenholt church. The oldest
parts are the north wall of the nave and the
west doorway, dating from the end of the
12th century. St Mary's was largely restored
in 1851 to the design, it is said, of the curate,
the Rev J M Rawlings. The fourth church,

St. Peter's Church, Linkenholt

View into Wiltshire from Vernham Dean

Hurstbourne Tarrant

on the right, is *St Peter's, Hurstbourne Tarrant* which incorporates a mixture of styles: a beautiful Norman south doorway; 13th century aisles and a 14th century western bay. The tower was heightened with a spire in 1897, made partly of old timbers. On the north wall is a large mural, possibly 14th century representing the 13th century French legend of 'The three living and the three dead', where three kings out hunting met three skeletons which reminded them of their mortality. Another mural depicts the deadly sins.

The open country in the top left corner is the view looking out of Hampshire towards the Iron Age Hill Fort, Fosbury Camp. Just visible is *Dean Cottage* while a *hot air balloon* sails into the sunset. The *batsman* is wearing the colours of Linkenholt Cricket Club whose picturesque ground is situated opposite the church.

To the right of Vernham Dean church is *Vernham Manor House*, a fine Tudor building constructed round an E-shaped timber-framed structure. Extensive exterior alterations were carried out in 1960 and further refurbishment in the 1990s. Between the Manor and the church on its right is *The Square* in Hurstbourne Tarrant.

The *house* on the left was the village shop and post office but is now a private house. The imposing house across the road is *Four Winds Cottage*.

Winters can be very severe in this part of the valley and the wintry scenes are illustrated at the bottom. The *large house* in the corner is the brick and flint 'Always', Back Lane, Vernham Dean. It dates from the 17th century. The present owner says that the village carter lived there and remnants of the stable are in the garden. It was probably also, at one time, an ale-house. On the right is the *George Inn*. A bill of sale of the property in 1847 lists, among other things, 'thatched stable for seven horses, and piggeries adjoining, a flint and thatched granary . . . thatched barn . . . a skittle ground'.

Opposite the George is the *village pump and drinking fountain*, still in working order. This is a good example of the Victorian foundryman's art, water being discharged from the mouth of a lion's head. Seen through the icicles is the thatched *Beeches Farmhouse*. The 18th century timber-framed structure is now masked by rendering. In the kitchen is a large brick bread oven. The house was once a doctor's surgery, and operations were performed on the kitchen table.

The building on the right of the icicles was the *Post Office Stores* at Upton. When the panel was designed it was still functioning but is now a private house. The horse in front is *'Bearcone'* from a local stable. Bearcone was especially fond of Polo mints and would always stop hopefully by the shop. In the bottom corner is *Murrle Cottage* with the *River Swift* in full flood in springtime.

Lower border

Ferns (from the old village name Fernham); *snowdrops, hedgehog; primroses, badger and fungi, periwinkles, pheasant; dog rose, rabbit, blackberries; thistle*, with the names of the five villages.

The River Swift at Upton

Tangley
Hatherden
Wildhern
The Appleshaws
Penton

TANGLEY, HATHERDEN, WILDHERN, THE APPLESHAWS and PENTON

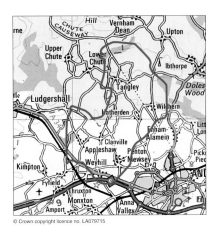

© Crown copyright licence no. LA079715

TANGLEY, HATHERDEN, WILDHERN

The parish of Tangley, which includes the hamlets of Hatherden and Wildhern, is situated in the north west corner of Hampshire, most of it in an officially designated 'Area of Outstanding Natural Beauty'. Icknield Way, the Roman road from Winchester to Cirencester, runs through the parish.

Top border

A Roman soldier; coat of arms of the Merceron family which held the title of Lord of the Manor; *an old well* 185 feet deep, reputed to be 350 years old, still used by the water authority to measure the water table; *arms of James Samborne* who endowed Hatherden School; *farm worker* with pitch fork.

Middle section

In the top left-hand corner is the *church of St Thomas of Canterbury*, Tangley, rebuilt in 1872 on the site of an earlier church. The tolling bell is believed to have been cast in 1522 while the early 17th century font is the only lead font in Hampshire. The tower and spire were built by Mr F Merceron in 1898 to commemorate Queen Victoria's diamond jubilee. In the *carriage* on the way to church is Mr Michael Colvin MP, of Tangley House, with his daughter who was married when the panel was being planned. Below the church at the crossroads is the *War Memorial*.

At the bottom left is *Christ Church, Hatherden*, built in 1857. In 1975 it was struck by lightning and completely gutted. A new church was built within the old walls and was rededicated by the Bishop of Winchester in 1977. In the centre of the panel is the *village hall at Wildhern*, built in 1959, and the *playing field*. To the right of the hall is the *Methodist Chapel* built in 1880 from flint and locally made bricks, replacing a nearby earlier building.

The white faced building to the left of the hall is *Hatherden Cottage* and, partly hidden on its left, *Oak Cottage*, home of Mrs Griffin who designed the panel. Its TV aerial is the only one in the Test Valley Tapestry. Between the hall and Hatherden Church is *Hatherden C of E School*, founded

Arms of Hatherden School

in 1725 by James Samborne for 24 poor children. To the left of the original building is a Victorian extension and, just in view, a modern classroom. Income from a Samborne Foundation still benefits the school and ex-pupils. The *'lollipop lady'*, Sheila Webb, sees children safely across the road. Other houses in the panel are typical of various kinds in the three villages. The *red telephone kiosk* has since been replaced by a modern type while the *low building* behind the *copper beech tree* represents intensive poultry farming. In the bottom left corner is *Maurice Hancocks with Friesian cows*.

Lower border

Woodpeckers caused considerable damage to the shingles on the spire of Tangley Church; there are at least two local *badger* setts; *deer*; a *hen*, representing the poultry industry; *grapes* – there are two local vineyards.

THE APPLESHAWS

The name Appleshaw is derived from Old English 'scarga' – a shaugh or wood; thus Appleshaw may mean 'apple wood'. It includes the hamlet of Ragged Appleshaw, the 'ragged' possibly being a corruption of 'roe gate' – the gate of the Royal Deer Forest of Chute. The northern boundary of the parish is the Wiltshire border.

Top border

The *sheep and the shepherds' crooks* are reminders of the annual Appleshaw Fair which was originally held three times a year: in May for the sale of pigs, and in October and November principally for sheep. In 1801 15,000 sheep were sold at the fair. Local farmers profited by growing turnips for the drovers and dealers.

Middle section

In the top right-hand corner is the church of *St Peter-in-the-Wood* built in 1836. In the centre of the panel is the *Walnut Tree Inn* named for the walnut trees which have long been associated with the village. In 1953 fifteen more were planted to mark the Queen's coronation. To the left of the public

The watch repairer at work in Appleshaw

Church of St Peter-in-the-Wood, Appleshaw

The clock at Appleshaw

Lucinda Green

house is the *village shop and post-office*. Tucked round the corner behind the thatched, bay-windowed cottage on the right is *Forge Cottage*, formerly the blacksmith's shop. A *cricket match* is in progress on the recreation ground, with the *pavilion* in the background. Clutching his bat is the splendidly bearded figure of *Dr W G Grace* who played there at least twice. On July 15th 1870 he played for Danebury against West Hants, taking 11 wickets in the two innings but managing only to score 0 and 14 respectively. One 'six', however, soared over the Ragged Appleshaw Road into Farmer Bailey's field where a thorn tree (now built over) was planted to mark the spot.

On the other side is *Lucinda Green*, formerly Prior-Palmer, the 1982 world champion of three-day eventing, who lives in the village. She is seated on her horse '*Be Fair*'.

In the corner are white *Beersheba daffodils* with their long, narrow trumpets. The bulbs were grown by the Revd G H Engleheart who lived in the village in the late 19th century. Beersheba bulbs, which were reputedly sold to Holland for about £1,000, can still be seen in local gardens.

Lower border

An *apple tree*, symbol of the village; a hoard of *Roman pewter vessels* was unearthed in the parish by the Revd Engleheart in 1897. The find comprised 10 large circular dishes together with numerous other items; they are now in the British Museum; the *local farrier*; a *walnut tree*, one of those planted to commemorate the coronation.

PENTON

Penton ('the farm at a penny rent'), with probably Saxon origins, comprised the twin parishes of Penton Mewsey and Penton Grafton. The Mewsey and Grafton are post-Conquest additions deriving from Maisy and Grestain in Normandy.

Top border

The *arms of the Stonor family* who held the manor from 1346. The *Sanctus Bell* inscribed 'Sic nomen Domini benedictum Ao Xi 1555'. It was discovered in a niche in the wall of the rectory during repairs in 1845, probably having been hidden there during the religious upheavals; a *wooden spade*, typical of those made at Penton for sale at the nearby Weyhill Fair; the *arms of Phillipa Roet* who married Geoffrey Chaucer the poet (1340-1400). Their grand-daughter inherited land locally.

Middle section

In the top left corner is *Holy Trinity Church* probably built in the mid 14th century by the Stonor family to replace an earlier church, mentioned in the Domesday Survey which possibly fell into decay during the

Black Death. The surrounding trees are symbolic of many fine local specimens. The knight on the splendidly caparisoned steed represents *Sir Robert de Maisy*, a descendant of the Robert who accompanied Duke William to Hastings in 1066. Sir Robert held the manor from 1233 to 1295 for his liege lord the Earl of Gloucester.

The centre section represents the main section of the village street which ends in a cul-de-sac, giving it a welcome measure of peace and quiet. Outside one of the houses is *a tractor*, symbolic of the village's continuing agricultural heritage. On its left is the sign of the village public house the *White Hart*. The first mention of an 'alehouse' in Penton occurs in the Court Roll of 1431.

In the right-hand corner is a *cast-iron hand pump*, typical of several that survive in gardens in the village. Between it and the inn sign is the prominent *village pond*.

Lower border

On the left is the *small bridge* spanning the stream which usually rises from springs beneath the pond and joins the Pillhill brook at Charlton. On its right are *wild flowers* and *ears of corn*.

Daffodils by Penton Pond

Smannell
Knights Enham
Enham Alamein
Charlton

SMANNELL, KNIGHTS ENHAM, ENHAM ALAMEIN and CHARLTON

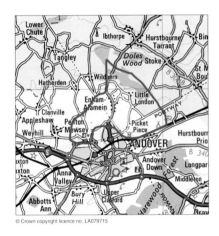

© Crown copyright licence no. LA079715

Smannell

SMANNELL

The name Smannell is thought to mean 'The place of the swineherds', a clearing in the forest where pigs were encouraged to grub out trees and undergrowth. There has been a settlement at Smannell and nearby Woodhouse since earliest times. The Saxons lived here and the Romans before them built two of their main highways through this district, the Portway and Harroway. Now, five roads meet in the centre of the village by the British Oak Inn.

Top border

Skittles, representing the annual village fete and bowling for the pig competition held before the war at Finkley House and then at Postgrove House. Since 1976 skittles competitions at Woodhouse Farm have raised money for charity; the *fifty-pence coin* commemorates Mr Christopher Ironside of Church Farm House who designed Britain's first decimal coinage introduced in February 1971; the *steam engine 'Lincoln Imp'*. This was owned by the People family who ran their threshing tackle business from Jubilee House. The 'Imp', fully restored, is exhibited at steam rallies by its owner, Derek Marder; the *cottage loaf and peel* denote bread making

begun at Woodhouse Bakery nearly two centuries ago and still in production. Until a coke-fired oven was installed in 1920 brushwood served as fuel; *Riding for the Disabled*: The Andover group started at Woodhouse Farm in 1972 with children from Icknield School; the *hurdle* represents three local businesses which supplied hurdles, peasticks, bean rods, faggots and logs. Birch twigs were sent to Crosse and Blackwell for colouring vinegar and bark from felled trees went to tanneries. There is still a fencing business at Little London.

Middle section

The *cottages* in the top left corner are from the hamlet of Little London which was established in 1665 by refugees from the great plague. The *cultivated fields* belong to Woodhouse Farm whose *farmhouse* (on the right) dates from 1746. *Thatched wooden barns* resting on staddle stones were destroyed when incendiary bombs were dropped on the village by a German bomber during the Battle of Britain in September 1940. The thatched building on the left is the *Woodhouse Bakery* which was originally three cottages (about 1640), housing workers engaged in charcoal burning in the surrounding woods. The *red bakers' van*

28

can be detected at the end of the cottage. The *cows* are part of the local herd of Friesians. The *staddlestones* with flowers at their base are from Finkley Manor Farmhouse (1787) which lies astride the Roman Portway. Finkley (from the old English for 'clearing of finches'), was recorded in medieval documents as a woodman's hut in the King's Andover Forest.

The red-tiled building is the *school*, built in 1873 for £324.15.6 and opened with 84 pupils whose ages ranged from 3 to 13. It is now a Church of England Primary School serving Smannell and Enham. Between the school and the church is the distinctive *post box*. *Christ Church, Smannell*, with its decorated brick and flint walls, was designed by the architect W White who also designed Hatherden Church. Both churches were consecrated by the Bishop of Winchester on the same day in November 1857, Smannell at 10.30 am. and Hatherden at 2.30 pm. A fine organ and wall paintings were given in 1890 by the Earle family of Enham Place. The original pews, riddled with woodworm, were recently replaced by oak pews made at the Enham Alamein workshops. The *mother and toddler* next to the *rider* in the bottom corner represent the drug rehabilitation unit at nearby Ashley Copse. A new mother and baby unit was opened here by the Princess of Wales in 1988, which accounts for the *red helicopter* of the Queen's Flight at the top of the panel.

Lower border

Animals and plants of the countryside; *primroses* and *rabbit*; *blackberries*; *pheasant*; an *oak branch*, representing the village inn, the British Oak.

Little London

KNIGHTS ENHAM, ENHAM ALAMEIN

The prefix 'Knights' in the name dates from the 13th century when the manor was in the possession of the Knights Hospitallers, more commonly known as the Knights of St John. 'Alamein' was added after World War II when the people of Egypt presented £225,000 for the building of Alamein Village, and three pairs of wrought-iron gates in gratitude for their deliverance from the Axis powers after the Battle of Alamein in October 1942, which turned the tide of war in favour of the Allies.

White Cottage, Enham Alamein

Top border

Two books representing Enham's book-binding industry; the *insignia of the Mediterranean Fleet 1942*, the *8th Army* (Desert Rats) and the *Western Desert Air Force* which are featured in the three stained glass windows in the Alamein Church of St George; a *basketful of flowers* representing the combined Enham industries of basket making and the garden centre.

Middle section

The large building at the top of the panel is the *Enham Resource Centre* for assessing the

Candle-making

disabled, completed in 1990 and opened by the Patron, H.R.H. the Duchess of Gloucester. The complex, funded entirely by voluntary sources, is the most recent addition to the facilities of Enham Village Centre since its inception just after World War I. The story of the Village Centre began in 1916 when there was concern about the increasing number of men being disabled on the Western Front. A group of people envisaged the creation of a number of Village Centres where such men could find rest, treatment and recuperation as they trained to cope with their disabilities.

In October 1918 Enham Place, a private estate with houses, cottages, buildings and 1,027 acres, was acquired. Exactly a year later Enham Village Centre, planned as the first (but destined to be the only one) of its kind, was officially opened and welcomed the first intake of fifty men.

A medical block had been presented by the British Red Cross Society, and workshops donated by various towns. Training started in horticulture, farming, forestry, woodcraft, poultry rearing, electrical fitting, basket-making, carpentry and joinery, boot and shoe repairing, cookery and rural wood industries, including furniture making.

30

Within three years more than 1,000 severely disabled ex-servicemen had received training and careful medical attention. In 1926 an old hut, the village entertainment centre was replaced by the Landale Wilson Institute, given by Mr and Mrs D Landale Wilson to mark their silver wedding anniversary.

Enham's workshops played a significant part in Britain's war effort between 1939 and 1945, including the manufacture of glider carcasses. Today, the centre continues to flourish; living accommodation has been improved, while the range of industries has developed and now includes a furniture division and an electronics division. The new Resource Centre includes work, training, education and occupational therapy areas with supporting medical and care facilities, together with Enham's main Occupational Workshop. The *cedar tree* in front of the building is now the logo of the Enham Trust.

The *biplane* in the upper corner symbolises the link between World War I and the manufacture of glider parts in World War II. Below the Resource Centre, on the left, is an *elm tree*, one of many, most of which are now, sadly, lost. The *17th century thatched White Cottage* houses the estate office and a

museum of the Battle of Alamein. *Silver birches* separate this from *St George's, The Alamein Church*, consecrated by the Rt Rev Colin James, Bishop of Basingstoke, on St George's Day 1974. A small private chapel owned by Enham Village Centre, known as St George's Chapel, previously stood on the site. The Alamein Memorial Chapel, which attracts visitors from all over the world, is dedicated to those who took part in the Battle. Below the elm tree is the *bus shelter*, originally a shepherd's hut and rebuilt brick by brick. In front is a *flower stall*, representing the Garden Centre. The building in the centre is *The Landale Wilson Institute*. To its right is the *general store* and *sub-post office*. The disabled are represented by a *lady in a wheelchair and friend*, also emphasising the social aspect provided by the store. In front of the Landale Wilson hall is a *bed of red roses* planted as a memorial to the late Medical Officer Dr MacCullum.

Below the rose garden is *Bradbury House*. Formerly called the White House and used as the village administrative centre, it is now eight flatlets for disabled people. The conservatory has been demolished. In the bottom left corner is the 12th century church of *St Michael, Knights Enham*, depicted with lighted windows to represent its warmth and

constant availability. The *squirrel* in the tree denotes its country setting; a *hedgehog* sits in front. The *imposing gates* in the bottom corner are one of the set of three presented by the Egyptian government. Surrounding the gates are some of the abundant *flora and fauna* including daisies, fly agaric fungus, cuckoo pint, cowslip, bluetits, butterfly and snail. The *poppy* represents the war dead. The huge *candle* made in the workshops is now listed in the Guinness Book of Records. It was 101.7 feet tall and was exhibited at the Andover Show in 1989.

Lower border

Fox, badgers in their sett; *ferns, leaves, robins, ladybird butterflies* and *sheep*.

CHARLTON

There is evidence of Saxon settlement at
Charlton but it was only in the 1980s that it
achieved recognition as a separate parish,
having previously been part of Andover.
Nearby Foxcotte, on the other hand, was
a thriving little village long before the
Conquest with its own chapel. Over the
years there was a movement of population
from Foxcotte to Charlton, possibly dating
from the Black Death.

Top border

Artefacts and a dwelling, representing
Charlton's Saxon heritage. During
excavations carried out at Old Down Farm
in the 1970s evidence of houses of the
period was discovered together with various
weapons, implements and items of jewellery;
the *Charlton Mace Head*: this rare stone mace,
dating from somewhere between 5600 to
1800 BC, was found in May 1969 by Mr A F
Glover in his garden at Foxcotte Close; the
oak tree planted to commemorate Queen
Victoria's Diamond Jubilee in June 1897; the
bell presented to the church of St Thomas,
Charlton, by Lady Susan Sutton of Penton
Lodge on its consecration in March 1908;
symbols representing 'livelihoods'; a horse shoe

and arable farming; the school, and a baker
representing the Hopgood family whose
business goes back over 100 years.

Middle section

Just left of centre at the top of the panel is
Marchment Farm, with grazing sheep, a
horse and farm buildings. To the right of
the farm is *Foxcotte Tower*. In 1853 Miss
Martha Gale (following the example of her
uncle Dr Goddard, who had demolished the
old church of St Mary, Andover and rebuilt
it), pulled down the ancient building of
Foxcotte Chapel and rebuilt it. In 1907, with
the population of Foxcotte down to 33, the
decision was taken to remove the church
building from Foxcotte to Charlton but the
great opposition dictated that the tower
should remain where it was. In the early
1970s it was extended and made into an Arts
and Crafts Centre, and in due course it was
bought by a London artist for use as an art
gallery. It now serves as a play school. The
houses to the right of the tower represent
those built to meet the needs of the area.

The *lake* represents the very popular
Charlton Sports and Leisure Centre, built
on 76 acres of waste ground. In addition to
the boating and fishing lake, sports pavilions

Charlton Sports Centre

and children's play area depicted in the panel, there is also a superb all-weather athletics track and artificial hockey and football pitches. To its left is the thriving *village shop* and post office and across the road is the *church of St Thomas*. This stood at Foxcotte until Dr Frederick Preston, Vicar of Andover from 1902 to 1910, initiated the move to Charlton. Many people felt this was desecration and sacrilegious. Materials from the demolished church were taken in waggons to Charlton. The foundation stone was laid on 3rd March 1908 and consecration, conducted by the Bishop of Dorking, took place on 19th August of the same year.

The *Royal Oak public house* is prominent lower in the panel. It is thought that it began trading as a beer house in 1795 as 'The Three Cups'. In front of the pub is a thriving *flower stall* which was established in the village in 1989 while the *thatched cottages* at the bottom of the panel, located opposite Carters Meadows, are Bluebell Cottage on the left and Snowdrop Cottage on the right. They were once another public house, 'The Buck and Dog'.

Below the splendid *horse-chestnut tree* and *beds of daffodils* are the *watercress beds* which were still being harvested when the panel

was designed, but closed in 1993. The site has now been turned into a landscaped private fishing area.

Lower border

Local birds and fish found at Charlton Lakes – *Canada geese*; *moorhens*; *swift*, *martin* and *swallow*; *trout*, *chub* and *silver bream*.

Charlton Lakes

Andover

ANDOVER

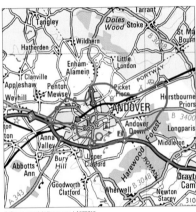

© Crown copyright licence no. LA079715

Andover, the largest town in the Test Valley Borough, has a population of 34,000. At the northern end of the district, it is 18 miles from Romsey and nearly 25 miles from the southern borders.

The unparished area of Andover includes Knights Enham and Enham Alamein. However, those two communities are depicted in a separate Tapestry along with Charlton and Smannell. Accordingly, the boundary line indicates the area covered by the respective Tapestries, and not the parish boundaries.

Andover developed around the crossing point of the River Anton, a tributary of the Test, and was a natural staging point for travellers along the Harroway, a prehistoric trackway, and the Portway, the Roman road running east and west. Small groups settled but all that really survives of those pre-Saxon times is the town's name: from 'Anna-dwfr', or 'Andefera', 'the river of the ash trees'.

When the kingdom of Wessex was established the Kings built their hunting lodges in the vicinity, near excellent hunting forest; traders arrived and the foundations of a prosperous town were laid. It became a chartered borough in 1178 when Henry II granted it the right of a Guild of Merchants. In stage-coaching days it was an important stop on the London-Exeter route, with several inns catering for the traffic, and was sometimes called 'The Gateway to the West'.

Its status as a quiet country market town changed dramatically from 1961 when the Andover Borough Council entered into an agreement with the Greater London Council and Hampshire County Council to move industry and people to Hampshire. New housing developments were planned to cater for a large increase in population, industrial estates were laid out and schools, shops, roads and other amenities followed. Then, under the Local Government Reorganisation of 1974, Andover, with Romsey and Stockbridge, became part of Test Valley District Council (later to become Test Valley Borough Council).

Top border

The *old Norman church* demolished by Dr Goddard in 1841. It replaced a Saxon church on the site, burned down in the great fire of 1141, and was reputed to be the largest and finest example in the country of a church of its kind, a spacious building, covering a much greater area than the present church. The tower had a lead-covered timber spire 80 feet high but this fell in a gale on 11 August 1705. In 1840 the building was lit by gas and had a congregation of 2,000. But Victorian passion for church building led to its destruction, despite the fact that many citizens bitterly resented the demise of their ancient but well loved church. In particular they resented the haphazard way in which fittings were disposed of. The communion table, for example, went to the Angel Inn. A local historian described the demolition of the church as 'an act of terrible vandalism'; the *confirmation of Olaf Tryggvason* by the Bishop of Winchester in Andover in 994. The previous year a Viking army in 94 ships, led by the Norwegian Prince Olaf and the Danish King Swegen, invaded England and attempted, in vain, to sack London. After 'burnings, harryings and killings' along the south coast the Viking forces regrouped for the winter at Southampton.

St Mary's, Andover

King Ethelred and his council negotiated with the invaders to supply them with provisions and 16000 pounds of silver in return for a commitment to cease harrying. The King, from his hunting lodge near Andover, sent Alfege, Bishop of Winchester, to bring Olaf to Andover 'with great ceremony'. Olaf, who had previously been converted by a hermit in the Scilly Isles, was confirmed again by the Bishop on the site of St Mary's Church. After the ceremony Ethelred gave Olaf gifts in return for a promise never to return to Britain. Olaf kept his promise and in 995 returned to Norway to convert his new kingdom to Christianity.

A *shepherd and sheep* representing Andover sheep fairs which were not as large as those at nearby Weyhill, but were of considerable local importance; *archery in Common Acre* where men were commanded to prepare for Agincourt. And after Agincourt, in 1542, Henry VIII introduced a form of 'national service' with men being compelled to take part in archery practice at the butts; *'Oliver Twist'* asking for more at Andover workhouse. This refers to the great 'Andover Scandal' of 1846 when a Parliamentary Select Committee probed the running of the workhouse under ex-Sergeant Major McDougal and his wife. The union work-

house in Junction Road was built in 1836 and McDougal, who had fought at Waterloo, and his wife were appointed as Master and Matron. The Board of Guardians set the inmates to grinding bones for fertiliser. The McDougals were dishonest and cruel had provided so poor a diet that inmates gnawed the bones for the marrow. A young London reporter, Charles Dickens, had covered similar inquiries for his paper and the idea of the Oliver Twist plot was conceived; the *Norman arch* which formed the west door of the old church was taken down and rebuilt on another site in the High Street. It is now known as 'Norman Gate'; a *bullock* representing the old cattle markets.

Brewer's dray at Town Mills

Middle section

The buildings in the middle of the panel on the left are the *Town Mills*. At the time of Domesday there were six mills in Andover. One of them, the Town Mill, in the centre of the complex, still straddles the river and is now a restaurant and public house. The main building in the panel is *the Guildhall*. There has been a Guildhall at the northern end of the High Street market place for centuries for the meetings of the town's governing bodies. One such building stood there from 1583 to 1724 and another from 1725 to 1825. The present Guildhall, constructed in Bath stone to the plans of John Harris, was built in 1825/26 at a cost of around £9,000. Furnishing it cost a further £600 and on 6 June 1826 the Corporation moved into the new Council Chamber. The Guildhall had two floors, the lower one open and arched for use by stallholders as a covered market.

Originally the building had a clock turret but that was removed in 1904. There were three flagpoles, one for the union flag, one for the Lord Lieutenant and one for the Borough. The *gas lamp standard* in the forecourt was erected to commemorate the Diamond Jubilee of Queen Victoria in 1897. Later consigned to a Council yard it was re-erected in 1977 to mark the Queen's Silver Jubilee. The Guildhall was refurbished in 1981.

Dominating the right hand side of the panel, as it does the town, is *St Mary's Church*, seen from Marlborough Street. The church was built by Dr William Stanley Goddard, Headmaster of Winchester College from 1793 to his retirement in 1809. He married an Andover heiress, Henrietta Gale. In 1835 the Vicar, the Rev Charles Ridding, and Dr Goddard decided that the church was too small for 'this agreeable little town' and that possibly the tower was unsafe. After Henrietta's death in 1830 Dr Goddard used his inherited wealth for local charitable purposes and he agreed to be the 'anonymous' benefactor for a new church. Plans were drawn up by a young architect Augustus Livesay whose design, in Victorian Gothic, was modelled on Salisbury Cathedral. The estimated cost was £9,437. The church was built of Caen stone shipped in by the Andover canal for a start in 1841. Work went well until 3rd June 1842 when the roof fell in causing the death of one workman. Two days later the south clerestory wall collapsed. Many Andoverians who resented the loss of the old church saw those incidents as evidence of divine disfavour.

Town Mills

St John's, formerly the Workhouse

Andover Guildhall at Christmas

Andover on market day

The first Divine Service in the new St Mary's was held on Sunday, 11th August 1844. The final demolition of the old church and the completion of the tower took until 1846 by which time the cost had risen to more than £20,000, well over double the original estimate. Sadly, Dr Goddard did not live to see the completion of his church, as he died on 10 October, 1845. Sir Nicholas Pevsner describes it as a 'very remarkable building' and the design 'extraordinary and quite brilliant'.

The large building below and to the right of the church is *Keens House*, in the old Town Station Yard, the original headquarters of the TSB Trust Company, which moved from London to Andover in 1973. As the work-force increased to more than 1500 it became Andover's largest employer and it supports the community in many ways. TSB Trust Company, subsequently renamed TSB Bank plc, expanded to occupy new offices in Charlton Place in 1986.

The imposing building in the bottom left corner is the listed *Savoy Chambers* in London Street which has been virtually rebuilt. Originally the Star and Garter inn it was first built in the 18th Century, and acquired in 1770 by the enterprising Heath family to become a focus for brewing and banking. In 1861 it was sold to Dr Jabez Elliott, a surgeon, who named it Elliott House. In 1934 it became Savoy Chambers and has been used by various local companies for office accommodation. The houses next to it are situated at the top of *Chantry Street*.

Centre bottom is the so-called *Round House*, one of the two tollhouses which served Andover. One was at the junction of Salisbury Road and Weyhill Road and the other at the Tavern crossroads for the collection of tolls from users of the turnpike roads. On the right of the Round House is the former Workhouse *St John's Hospital*, built in 1836 and still serving as an old peoples' unit when the Andover panel was designed. The building is now part of the Cricklade College complex, with a teaching block, tutorial rooms and the teachers' centre. The long building in the bottom corner is the *War Memorial Hospital* in Charlton Road. After the Great War in 1918 a new hospital was proposed and a committee chaired by Dr E A Farr, Medical Officer of Health for Andover, was set up to raise the estimated cost of £16,000. The first town Carnival in 1924 brought in £1,300 and soon the total amount, a considerable sum in the twenties, was raised.

Work began in 1925. The War Memorial
Hospital was opened on 30th June 1926 by
Field Marshal the Viscount Allenby. The
first name in the Visitors' Book is that of
H.R.H. Edward, Prince of Wales, later King
Edward VIII. He combined a visit to the
hospital with an engagement the previous
day when he had opened the Landale
Wilson Institute in Enham Village Centre.

Lower border

*Wild dog rose; grebe; daffodil; fox; ducks; poppy;
badger; wild arum; owl; toadstools; hedgehog;
brimstone butterfly; violet; chalk hill blue
butterfly; viper or adder.*

View towards Andover

Thruxton
Fyfield
Kimpton

THRUXTON, FYFIELD and KIMPTON

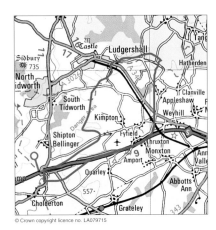

© Crown copyright licence no. LA079715

These three villages lie in a triangle within a mile or so from each other just north of the busy A303 to the west.

THRUXTON

Five miles from Andover, Thruxton was almost certainly one of four 'Annes' named in the Domesday Book under the Andover Hundred. In the 12th century the name was Turkilleston which, over the centuries, changed via Thruckleston (16th century), Throxton (18th century) to the present form. Gliders flew to Arnhem from the World War II airfield to the west of the village. Now Thruxton is nationally known as a motor racing centre. Unlike the racing circuit, the village can hardly be seen from the main road. In 1985 the centre of the village was declared a Conservation Area.

Top border

Racing car, representing the Thruxton Racing Circuit, which opened on the airfield in March 1968 and is the home of racing run by the British Automobile Racing Club; *arms of Lisle impailing Courtenay*. Sir John Lisle who died in 1407 is buried in the churchyard. His magnificent brass in the church, one of the best examples of the earliest type of joined chain mail armour, carries his own arms with those of his wife, Elizabeth. His feet rest on a lion and part of the brass is depicted in the lower border; *carrier's cart* of Mr E Piper. Mr Piper lived at Flint House and operated as the village carrier with his wagonette and horse, taking goods and passengers between Thruxton, Andover and Salisbury. Behind the wagon is one of the *buses* of the Amport and district Bus Company which now provides local services.

Middle section

In the top left hand corner is the *parish church of St Peter and St Paul*, tucked away off School Lane beside the manor house. Parts date from the 13th and 15th centuries but most of the present church dates from a 19th century restoration. Its treasures are the tombs and effigies of some of the lords and ladies of the manor, especially two 13th century coffin slabs and a 17th century wooden effigy of Elizabeth Philpott, lady of the manor, who was buried in 1616. Sadly, it is badly battered but her fashionable clothes are beautifully carved. Not visible to the public is the oldest bell, given in 1581, which was rung to warn of the coming Armada.

The original manor was destroyed and no trace remains but the *present manor*, built probably in the first half of the 18th century, is featured below the church. In front of the house is a fine *horse chestnut tree*. In the centre is another fine tree, a *sycamore*, planted by the Rev H D Baker to commemorate the birth of his son. At its foot is an old *milestone* which was moved to the village from the A303, the old turnpike road. The inscription gives the mileage to London as LXVIIII (69), not the normal LXIX, and to Andover V (5).

Inside the thatched wall in the centre, dating from the 17th century, is *Manor Cottage*, with the four windows. The white building behind Manor Cottage is the *Rectory* which was completed in 1837 by the Rev Donald Baynes. He also built the school in 1836, and each day boys would go to draw water from the pump room in the Rectory for the school. The Rectory was also the home of Dorothy Kerin, a faith healer of renown, who lived with the Rev Langford James in the early 1920s.

The *blue cottage*, a former cobbler's shop from which a Mr Scrivens sold pots and pans, was restored in the early 1970s since when it has been a very attractive feature of the village. Next to it is *Bray Cottage*, formerly

the village bakery and general stores. The Bray family were bakers in Thruxton until 1969 and their excellent bread was delivered over a wide area. The thatched roof was destroyed by fire in 1985. At the top of the panel are *Robins Roost and Forge Cottage* built in the 17th century of chalk and flint. In the past Robins Roost served the village as a laundry while the adjacent Forge Cottage was formerly known as School Cottage until the blacksmith's son, Ernest Lansley, took over his father's business and moved to Forge Cottage where horses were shod and wooden wheels were bound.

Lower border

This depicts the famous *snowdrops* and *primroses* which are a special feature of the village; the *name Turkilleston*. Turkil was a Saxon who had a 'tun', the Saxon word for 'farmstead' and later a hamlet or village. In the centre is part of the *brass of Sir John Lisle* in the parish church.

Aerial view of Thruxton airfield and circuit

Touring car racing at Thruxton Circuit

FYFIELD

The parish of Fyfield, which includes Redenham, is situated a few miles west of Andover, near the Wiltshire border. It was once a mere handful of thatched cottages with three large houses, the Manor, the Grange and the Rectory.

Top border

Section of the Roman pavement excavated in the 19th century and now in the British Museum. As can be seen, it incorporates a reference to the local family of Bodeni.

Toby Balding's racing yard at Fyfield

The excavations were carried out on Lambourne's Hill where other finds included a Roman hypocaust and pottery in 1830 and a range of four rooms in 1850; *arms of William Maudit* who held the manor, reduced to 3 hides, from 1086; *Rev Henry White*, former Rector of Fyfield, with his pitchpipe. His brother, the celebrated naturalist Gilbert White, wrote to his friend Daines Barrington from Fyfield on 12 February, 1771: 'My musical friend (i.e. his brother Henry) at whose house I am now visiting has tried all the owls that are in his near neighbourhood with a pitchpipe set at concert pitch and finds that they all hoot in B flat'; *the tug-of-war* across the Pillhill Brook between teams from Fyfield and Kimpton as part of the celebrations marking the Queen's Silver Jubilee in 1977.

Middle section

In the centre is the *Church of England School*, attended by pupils from all three villages. A plaque records the official opening: 'Dedicated by Faulkner Alison, Lord Bishop of Winchester, 21st September, 1966. Replaces Church of England schools in Fyfield, Thruxton and Kimpton which were founded in 1818, 1836 and 1872'. It was built to accommodate 70 pupils but two extra classrooms have since been added. *The child skipping* in front of the school is Karen, the grand daughter of Mrs Kathleen Pennells who embroidered this piece and who used strands of Karen's own hair for the hair in the tapestry. Also near the school is the *old school bell* from the former Fyfield National School, now a private residence, 'Bell Cottage'.

At the top the name of the village is shown on a *banner being towed by a plane*. Recording that planes carrying advertising banners often took off from Thruxton airfield and flew over the area. On the left is the *village post box* and the traditional *red telephone kiosk* which was there when the panel was worked but has since been replaced by steel and glass.

On *Walnut Tree Green* to the right, is the *village shop* and a representative *new house*. The magnificent display of *daffodils* were bought with village funds and planted by children in 1983.

Fyfield is known throughout the racing world as the home of G B (Toby) Balding, the racehorse trainer with two Grand National and many other wins to his credit. The *string of racehorses* represents those seen at exercise through the village in early mornings. His Grand National winners were Highland Wedding in 1969 and Little Polvier in 1989. The *pub sign* was changed to *Highland Wedding* to commemorate the victory. The small *church of St Nicholas* lies out of sight of the village street, down a lane next to the Manor. It dates from the 13th century but, like so many others, was extensively 'restored' by Victorian enthusiasts. Both pitchpiping Rev Henry White and his wife are buried in the churchyard. There is a *memorial oak tree* to Brigadier Simpson.

Bottom right hand is *Littleton Manor*. Littleton was once a separate village and at the time of Domesday was larger than either Fyfield or Kimpton but all that now remains are the Manor and Forge Cottage, home of Gillian Yarde-Leavett, one of the panel's designers. The other manor, Redenham, is represented by their *green village pump* seen above the church.

Lower border

Racehorse; a *heron*; some *ducks* and *geese* in front of Littleton.

Parish church, Kimpton

KIMPTON

Kimpton, source of the Pillhill Brook, six miles west of Andover, is a picturesque village with a number of thatched cottages, and even a thatched bus shelter. The main part of the village is clustered around the green while the other end had the school, now demolished, and now the village hall. It is known for the discovery at Karlis corner in 1966, by local archaeologist Max Dacre, of a Bronze Age cemetery. The farmer, William Flambert, cooperated by leaving part of the field uncultivated for four years during the extensive 'dig'. The archaeologists found evidence of 108 cremation burials in pottery urns up to 3500 years old to about 800 BC. All the finds are now in the British Museum.

Top border

The *other half of the Silver Jubilee tug-of-war* featured in the Fyfield panel, with the difference that the end of the Kimpton rope is looped round a tree!; the *crossed keys of St Peter and St Paul*, representing the parish church; *memorial on the north wall of the church to Robert Thornburgh* who died in 1522. Above the tomb which is half buried in the wall are two tablets. The lower one invites prayers for the souls of Robert and his wives and children. Above it is a brass relief of Robert in armour followed by brasses of his first wife and her two children and his second wife and her seven children; *urns* representing the excavations at Karlis Corner.

Middle section

At the top of the panel is a *field of stubble* after harvest at Poplar Farm. In the centre is *Garden Cottage*, one of the thatched houses which give such charm to the village, and, top right, the *Little Stranger* public house, formerly the New Inn. In the centre on the left is the *old thatched barn*, now a private residence, and on the right, on the green, the *thatched bus shelter*. Nearby, walking her dog Dolly, is *Mrs Gertie Coster*, a familiar figure when the panel was worked but, sadly, no longer living. Above her is the old *cast iron village pump*. The *signpost* at the road junction is also of cast iron. Above the sign post and the bus shelter is another thatched cottage, *Kimpton Cottage*.

Prominent is the *parish church of St Peter and St Paul*, situated behind Kimpton Manor and reached via a grass path. The present church was built in stages over a century and a half, from 1220 to 1370. It has had restorations but apart from the tower, no major structural alterations and it is therefore unified and harmonious. The original tower had become dangerous and was rebuilt between 1837 and 1839. The altar in the Shoddesden chapel on the north side of the church is the village war memorial. The small *daphne tree* depicted in the panel in the churchyard was planted in memory of Daphne Norman (nee Wise) who died at the age of 23 in 1982. The fine *copper beech tree* stands at the entrance to the churchyard.

To the right of the church is *Kimpton Manor*, previously the Rectory. A century ago the Rector moved out to a new Rectory built on higher ground as he suspected that there could well be drainage problems there. In 1995 he was proved right as, in the worst floods in living memory, a number of people have had to have their drains pumped out. An interesting feature of the Manor House is that the Deeds stipulate that wild bees in the end wall must be preserved. The *weeping willow* outside the manor was planted by Mrs Joan Pool in memory of her son Anthony who was killed in 1969 while hunting. Sadly, the tree was blown down during the great gale of 1987. In the bottom righthand corner is a fine *horse chestnut tree* with a *cow and calf* grazing by the Pillhill Brook.

Lower border

Some of the *cattle and sheep* on local farms and the family of *black kittens* which roamed Manor Farm Yard when the tapestry was being planned.

Wild flowers by Pillhill Brook

**Weyhill
Shipton Bellinger
Tidworth**

WEYHILL, SHIPTON BELLINGER and TIDWORTH

© Crown copyright licence no. LA079715

WEYHILL

For nine centuries until the 1950s, Weyhill was the venue of one of the most celebrated country fairs in Britain. The site was at the crossroads of two ancient trading routes, one from Cornwall to Kent (The Harrow Way) along which Cornish tin was carried, and the other ('the Gold Road') from Holyhead to Christchurch Bay, along which Irish gold was brought for shipping to the continent.

Originally held on Old Michaelmas Day and lasting for about a week, the fair was renowned for its enormous sales of sheep and hops. In its heyday horses, cheese and leather were also sold. It served as a hiring fair for servants and farm labourers and inevitably took on the nature of a pleasure fair. In Thomas Hardy's 'The Mayor of Casterbridge' Weyhill Fair became Weydon Priors where Henchard sold his wife and child for five guineas.

Now, with the demise of the fair, Weyhill is a quiet place three miles from Andover, bypassed by the main trunk road to the west.

Top border

Shows items associated with the fair: *The Weyhill Ghost*: folklore has it that a west country hop merchant named Leadbetter, arriving late at the Star Inn, was allocated the ostler's room. He was awakened by a noise on the stairs and saw a tall, gaunt figure with a candle in one hand and a butcher's knife in the other. The figure approached the bed, shook Leadbetter by the shoulders and drew the knife several times across his throat. He put the light on the table and left. Later in the night the awesome visitor returned with the knife, smeared with blood.

Terrified, Leadbetter fled and stammered his story to the landlord. But the ostler arrived to reveal the apparition was a deaf and dumb man who had been given orders to wake him at 4 o'clock to remind him that he had a pig to kill. A popular ballad, about 'The Weyhill Ghost' had a wide circulation; *sheep bells*, symbolising the sheep fair; *'horning the colt'* an ancient ceremony held at The Star and other locations. A newcomer to the fair, a 'colt', was initiated by the 'horning' rite. He was seated and a hat surmounted with two horns between which was fixed a cup, was placed on his head. Various verses with the chorus 'Horns, boys, horns; horns, boys, horns, and drink like his daddy, with a large pair of horns', were then sung while the cup was filled with ale which the colt had to drink, afterwards paying for half a gallon of ale for the assembled company; *hops and cheeses* sold at the fair.

Middle section

The *church of St Michael* is in the top left corner. A church at Weyhill is mentioned in the Domesday Book but the oldest part of the present church, the chancel arch, dates from the end of the 12th century. In 1506 ten oaks were sold from Ramridge wood for 8s 4d for roof repairs while in 1822 the lead on the roof was sold (over 3 tons for £64) and replaced by Welsh slates. The church was largely restored in the middle of the 19th century. The base of the cross in the church-yard is 13th century but the cross itself was brought from Jerusalem and added in 1904.

Weyhill Lodge to the right of the church has been converted into luxury flats. In the corner is part of the *yard and a crane* of A J Dunning and Son (Weyhill) Ltd on the old fairground site. The building firm was started in Penton by Alfred James Dunning in 1917, his son Victor being in the business from the

Mural at the Weyhill Fair inn

Detail - Sheep Fair and old Sun Inn

very beginning. The firm's premises moved to the site of the old sheep fair in 1921 and the business flourished establishing an enviable reputation in the diverse fields of property development, construction work, shopfitting, scaffolding over a very wide area and, more locally in undertaking and farming. It became a limited company in 1936. In post-war years, Dunnings played its part in the redevelopment of Andover. It was, however, a victim of the recession, going into receivership in December 1989. Parts of the firm still continue under a new name, and at Weyhill Farm.

The *houses below the church* include council houses, Barrett homes and an old folk's bungalow. The *thatched building* across the road, originally two cottages, is now a farm house. The *horse and rider* going over the jump in the centre are a reminder of the riding stables run by Mrs Hartigen at Homestead, now a nursing home. Horse trials and point to point races were held locally. The *row of cottages* below the rider are owned by the Parish Council and were originally for the poor of the parish but are now let. Across the road is *Ramridge House* on whose land the greater part of Weyhill Fair was once held. For years it was used as a furniture store for Dunnings but was later

St Michael's, Weyhill

sold for conversion to flats. The *cows* in the bottom right corner represent local mixed farming, while in the opposite corner is the *village pond* with swan, mallard, coot and moorhen. The swan was used for the badge of the *village school* featured at the bottom of the panel. Built as a National School in 1855, with Miss Julia Hall as the Mistress, it was supported by public subscriptions and the 'children's pence'. Its one room was rather dark, with whitewashed walls but in 1897 the school was enlarged to accommodate 80 children. Sadly, because of falling numbers of children, it was forced to close in 1988.

Lower border

Catkins; *primroses, robin*; *hawthorn berries*; *hazel nuts*; *snowdrops*; *mushroom*; *deer* and *heron*.

SHIPTON BELLINGER

Inhabitants of Shipton Bellinger eked out a living for centuries on poor soil, barely six inches above the chalk in places; with little fertile farmland, sheep farming was the major livelihood and the village name comes from the Saxon 'Sceap Tun', or sheep farm. The parish, on the eastern edge of Salisbury Plain, is like a finger of Hampshire poked into Wiltshire. It was only when the Army came to Tidworth that the village began to develop as a dormitory area for the garrison. It is now a mixture of old and new.

At Domesday the village was recorded as Sceptone and Snodingstone, the two manors. The Bellinger connection was added in 1297 when Ingram Berenger became Lord of the Manor of Shipton.

Top border

The *three medieval bells of St Peter's Church* which have probably been rung since at least the late 16th century. All three are listed for preservation by the Council for the Care of Churches. The treble bell has the inscription 'Johannes Cristi care dignare pro bois orare' (John, beloved of Christ, deign to pray for us). The second is inscribed 'God be our Guyd

RB 1600'. The largest, the tenor, over three feet in diameter and weighing 9 cwt, is inscribed 'Sancte Nicolae ora pro nobis' (Saint Nicholas pray for us); the *mail coach* which ran daily from Marlborough to Salisbury in the early 19th century. It arrived at The Boot Inn with mail at 6.30 in the morning and returned at 6.30 in the evening; the *Ram* is the village symbol; *sign of The Boot*, the village inn.

Middle section

St Peter's Church is prominent at the top. There is evidence of a 10th century church in the village, although it is unlikely that anything remains. The present stone and flint church, with its stone windows and a wooden bell turret, was at least partly built in the 14th century and may have been restored three hundred years later. There was a well documented major restoration in 1879 at a cost of £1500, but there is a mystery regarding the churchyard. Contemporary reports reveal that the Churchwardens, Messrs Gilbert and Rumsey, 'lowered the Churchyard in some places as much as four or five feet', at their own expense. Churchwarden's accounts, however, show that money was paid from Church Funds for 71½ days' work in the churchyard.

The *village sign* was erected by the Parish Council in 1982, the date being added to the shield of the Berenger family, but when the sign was repainted the date was left out. The *sheep* reflect the age old tradition of sheep farming.

The *thatched cottage* on the left is Bramble Cottage in the High Street, the oldest house in the village and a listed building. Below it is the village's ivy-covered *post box*. The imposing house at the bottom of the panel is *Manor Farm House* the only one of the five village farms left. The rear of the building is old but the front is Victorian. The *pheasant* flying over the village is a reminder of local field sports practised in the north of the parish by the Officers' Shoot and in the south by Snoddington Manor Estate.

Lower border

Hedgehog; purple milk vetch (Astragalus Damcus) rare in Southern England; *lapwing; short-eared owl* (found on the Plain); *red admiral butterfly; primroses.*

Garrison Church at Tidworth

Piper of the 2nd Tank Regiment, Tidworth

TIDWORTH

When the Test Valley Tapestry was being worked the garrison town of Tidworth sat astride the Wiltshire border and the county boundary divided the town with only half, South Tidworth, being in Hampshire. Some buildings had their fronts in South Tidworth (Hants) and their backs in North Tidworth (Wilts). Now the whole of Tidworth is within Wiltshire following a review of local government boundaries.

Tidworth and its surrounding countryside has been a training ground for the British Army since 1902 when 42,000 acres were bought, including the Tedworth Estate, once the home of Thomas Assheton-Smith, a celebrated huntsman. Tidworth House, built in 1828-30 with its gracious grounds is now the splendid officers' club and nursing sisters' quarters, next to the arena where polo is played and the famous Tidworth Tattoo was staged until 1977.

At the time of Domesday Tedorde or Todeorde comprised North and South Tedworth, each with about 30 people and each containing three separate manors.

Upper border

Nuns' Walk and Nuns' Market. In 1164 Henry II granted the tithes of North and South Tidworth to the nuns of Amesbury and a charter for a weekly market. The nuns walked to Tidworth, giving rise to the name Nuns' Walk; the *Tedworth Drummer Boy*: in March 1661 William Drury, a Tidworth drummer, tried to obtain money in Ludgershall by subterfuge, using 'a counterfeit pass and warrant'. John Mompesson, the magistrate, confiscated his drum which was eventually sent to Mompesson's home, Tedworth House. Soon phantom drums rattled, loud scratching sounds were heard and 'there was violent beating and shaking of bedsteads'. These disturbances led to the first recorded poltergeist investigation when King Charles II sent his chaplain, the Rev. Joseph Glanvil, an authority on witchcraft, to investigate. He was unable to determine positively whether or not trickery was involved; a *mounted soldier* representing cavalry regiments associated with Tidworth; a *modern tank* and *helicopter*.

Middle section

Top left is *The Tower* or Observatory, built by the squire, Thomas Assheton-Smith so that his disabled daughter could watch the hunt. But it also had a further potential use. He had a barrel of tar installed on top of the tower to be lit if information was received of the approach of rioters bent on wrecking agricultural machinery. To the right of the tower is the little *Burial Chapel* in the woods, built using some of the material from the old South Tedworth Church which was demolished in 1784. The chapel was the only local place of worship until the church of St Mary the Virgin was built in 1880. It became very dilapidated but thanks to a generous legacy it has now been restored and is used for a monthly 'Songs of Praise' service and the occasional baptism.

Prominent at the top of the panel is *Tedworth House* built in 1828, when a former house on the site was demolished, and completed in 1830. The small house in the fork of the road is *the White Lodge*, built at the entrance to the drive of the big house and still occupied today. The red brick building to the left of the Lodge was the *Church of England School* endowed by Mrs Assheton-Smith in 1857. She 'clothed 16 scholars . . .

the sight of the girls in their red cloaks on a Saturday afternoon and of the noisy urchins rushing from the porch would suffice to gladden the heart'. The school was enlarged in 1903 to provide accommodation for 110 pupils but it was demolished in 1985 despite local attempts to have it preserved for a museum. There are now six schools serving the Tidworth area. The *red house* further up the road represents the station houses while to the right are *thatched cottages* by the old Reading Room on the border of North and South Tidworth. The *Reading Room* itself is alongside, in front of which is one of the old style *red telephone kiosks*.

The *factory type building* in the centre is the Royal Ordnance Depot which issues clothing and equipment to Army personnel. In front of the Depot is the *Royal British Legion Club* built on the site of an old cinema which was burnt down. Across the road is a *garage* which has subsequently been rebuilt as a modern petrol filling station.

Below the garage is the parish *Church of The Holy Trinity*. This 13th century building served North Tidworth but when the South Tidworth church was made redundant it became the parish church for the whole town. It is part of the United Benefice of

Tidworth, Ludgershall and Faberstown. Below the British Legion Club are two *cottages in Pennings Road*, the only two of a line left standing, while further down the road, in the left bottom corner, is the *Ram Inn*, the third of the same name on the same site. Opposite is a former *grocery shop and a post office*. Both have been demolished to make way for a new fish and chip shop and restaurant.

Lower border

Butterflies; *badger*; *sheep*; *hares and rabbits*; *squirrel*; *owl*; *pheasant*; *fox*; *hawthorn and blackberry bushes*; *corn field*; *the Tedworth Hunt*.

Monxton
Amport
Grateley

MONXTON, AMPORT and GRATELEY

© Crown copyright licence no. LA079715

Monxton village street

MONXTON

Monxton, with its attractive thatched cottages, is a long, narrow village spread along both sides of the Pillhill Brook. Its neighbours along the line of the brook are Amport to the west and Abbotts Ann and Anna Valley to the east.

Top border

The *arms of King's College Cambridge*. The manor of Monxton was included in the property that Henry VI granted to the college (originally the Royal College of the Blessed Mary and St Nicholas) when he founded it in 1441. There are many records of 'Monkestone' in the muniment room at King's; *Bec 1094 AD*. After the Conquest in 1066 the manor was granted to Hugh de Grandmesnil, a Norman baron, who then granted it to the Abbey of Bec-Hellouin in Normandy. The abbey held 'Anne de Bec', as it was then called, for the next 300 years. In 1404 Henry IV gave it to to his son John of Lancaster, constable of England, and when John died in 1435 it passed to Henry VI; *1920s*: King's college continued to be the corporate lord of the manor of Monxton and to own much property in the village until 1921 when it sold the properties under the hammer at auction.

Middle section

At the top is the *parish church of St Mary*. This was rebuilt in 1853-54 in brick and flint on the site of the medieval parish church, of which only the 12th century capitals of the chancel arch remain. There is a fine brass in the floor of the nave of a kneeling lady in Elizabethan dress with a man, also kneeling, behind her. The parson from 1723 to 1748 was Thomas Rothwell who was so devoted to mathematics that he would sit alone in his parlour to which not even members of his family were admitted. Occupying himself 'with figures and Algebra . . . that for many of the last years of his life he stirred not out of his house, no, not even to Church, but had a constant Curate . . . and gave himself not time to be shaved, but let his beard grow till he was a spectacle . . .' Flying near the church are *doves from the dovecot* on the right, from the forecourt of Monxton Manor. The row of *thatched cottages* along the village street are probably 17th century. At the end is the *Black Swan Inn* (commonly known as the Mucky Duck), which has been the village pub at least since the 17th century. The *old water pump* stands above one of the old village wells in the front garden of Well Cottage. The house on the other side of the road, with the large window, is *Hutchens Cottage*, formerly a farmhouse.

The *wall with the mill wheel* built into it is outside Monxton Mill. There was a mill here in 1086, worth 7s 6d at the time. *The bridge* is at the other end of the village over the Pillhill Brook which rises in Kimpton and then flows through Amport and Monxton before joining the River Anton near Upper Clatford. *A magpie* sits on the bridge. Also in the centre section are *Canada geese, kingfisher* and *local plants, leaves* and *flowers – lily, foxglove, lords and ladies, bullrushes* and *greater bladder-wort.*

Lower border

Duck; swan; water iris; frog, dragonfly; heron.

Monxton Cottages

Thatching

View along Pillhill Brook, East Cholderton

Stained glass window in Amport church

AMPORT

Amport is an irregular-shaped village in the valley of the Pillhill Brook, four miles west of Andover. It was called Anna in the Domesday Book; the source of this name may be Saxon ('ashtree') or possibly Celtic ('brook'). When William the Conqueror gave the manor to Hugh de Port it became Anne de Port which over the years changed to Amport.

Top border

The *badge of the RAF Chaplain's Department,* based in Amport House; *part of the coat of arms of the Sheppard/Routh family.* In 1801 Dr Thomas Sheppard, whose father was the wealthy Rector of Basingstoke, married Sophia Routh, a daughter of the Revd Peter Routh of Beccles and a woman with a keen social conscience. Thomas inherited substantial property in Amport from his father, a curate there, and when Thomas died it passed to Sophia. Thomas's Will stipulated that she should spend at least two months every year in Amport but she built a house and lived there for the rest of her long life, using her wealth for philanthropic purposes. In 1815 she built and endowed the school and six almshouses; *the symbol of the Paulets* who were prominent in the village

for generations. In 1649 Lord Henry Powlett purchased the manor of Amport. His great-great-grandson Charles who began rebuilding Amport House, which was completed in 1806, also changed the spelling of the family name from Powlett to Paulet, as the senior branch of the family had long done. As the 13th Marquis of Winchester he extended the estate to over 2000 acres; *motto of the almshouses 'for six poor widows AD 1815'*; another *part of the Sheppard Routh coat of arms.*

Middle section

At the top of the panel is *Amport House,* built by the 14th Marquis of Winchester in 1857 on the site of the mansion built by his father fifty years earlier. He demolished the farm buildings and cottages there, replacing them with extensive kitchen gardens, glass houses and orchards, putting up new cottages for his workers, and farm buildings half a mile away. During the time of the 16th Marquis (who died in 1962 aged one hundred), King Edward VII and Lily Langtry stayed at Amport House for the Stockbridge races and partridge shooting. The property is listed and has a garden designed by Gertrude Jeckyll. Amport House was requisitioned by the RAF in September 1939 and eventually bought by the Air Ministry to become the RAF Chaplains School. To the left is the *cricket field*.

On the right of the house is the *parish church of St Mary*, originally built about 1320-1330. In 1866 the church was restored with a rebuilt north transept, new north and south windows and the porch and vestry.

In the centre typical *Amport cottages* lead up to the *school*, which has served the village well for 180 years. The scene of Amport School pupils dancing round the *maypole on the green* is one of the most delightful features in the whole Tapestry. The green is used for the school's Dance Festival held every year on 12th May, continuing a tradition started by Mrs Sheppard. She had a maypole erected in her garden and invited all the children from the school to dance around it, giving them a penny and a currant bun. The celebration was held on Old May Day, 12th May instead of 1st May, and so it is to this day. By the *red telephone kiosk* opposite the school is the well-known figure of *Mrs Mac and her dog*.

In the bottom righthand corner is the *window of Grateley School* which could not be squeezed into the Grateley panel. This 'overlapping' is an example of happy

co-operation between the designers and the embroiderers of the two panels. The *flora and fauna* around the green are typical of those seen in the village. *Snowdrops* cover the church grounds in the Spring.

Lower border

Violets; *hazelnuts*; *ladybirds*; *primroses*; *holly and berries*; *grasses*, *hedgehog* and *roses* – all to be seen in abundance along the lanes.

St Mary's Church, Amport

Maypole dancing at Amport Green

St Leonard's, Grateley

The Plough Inn, Grateley

GRATELEY

Grateley in the north west corner of Hampshire derives its name from the 'greatnlea' or 'big wood clearing' to the southwest of the church. It is a village split into two distinct parts, one clustered around the church, Manor Farm and the Plough Inn, and the other a mile away around the railway built in the late 19th century.

Top border

The legend along the top of the border *'Laws for All England 925'*, refers to the council (or witanagemot) which the Saxon King Athelstan, self-styled 'King of the English' is reputed to have held here in 925, drawing up the first Code of Laws for all England. His enactments provided for a uniform coinage and dealt with the punishment of thieves. *Quarley's three historic church bells* are housed in a roofed, ground-floor frame alongside the church wall and are rung by hand from inside the church; *motifs* from some of the very old floor tiles, possibly from Clarendon Palace, now in the chancel of the church; the *shield* is from the coat of arms of the Maudit family, the first

prominent land-owners in Grateley in the 12th century; the *chain* is the symbol of St Leonard, patron saint of prisoners.

Middle section

Top left is *Quarley Hill*, site of an Iron Age fort, which overlooks the village. It is the only hill fort in Hampshire which has four entrances at opposite points, after the fashion of Roman camps and it could well have been here that Athelstan held his council. Below Quarley Hill are *commercial chicken houses* representing several hatcheries in the village. A *train* stands at *Grateley station*, now just a halt. When the railway was built the powerful Boutcher family did not relish the idea of having a station near their house in the village – so it was built a mile away. The road joining the two parts of the village was once a private road connecting the Boutcher's Grateley House to the station. Above the station is a *helicopter* on exercise from Middle Wallop.

Below the chicken houses is *St Leonard's Church*. The nave is mainly 12th century. The 13th century stained glass in one of the panels of the east window was 'rescued' from a restoration of Salisbury cathedral by the architect James Wyatt. He had thrown it in a ditch where it was spotted, retrieved and taken to Grateley.

Below the station are *postwar houses* while the *barn and grain silo* are at Manor Farm. The imposing *Plough Inn* in the centre of the village is featured on the centre right, with its fine specimen of a *horse-chestnut tree*, one of several planted to commemorate the Diamond Jubilee in 1897. Another, with pink 'candles', is in the bottom right-hand corner. *Swallows* perch on the wire above the *village store and post office*, on the right of which is *Hope Cottage*. Walking their dogs past the two cottages are *Mrs Harman and Mrs Holland*, familiar figures when the panel was being worked. *Farmer Peter Clarke* is seen in the bottom right-hand corner with one of his *shire horses*, a feature of the village – the public house near the station, formerly the Railway Hotel, is now called the Shire Horse. *Aylesbury ducks* swim on the pond while *yellow flag irises* and *lords and ladies* grow on the bank and *holly blue butterflies* flutter above. In the bottom left-hand corner is the entrance and doorway of *Grateley School*, with part of the building in the Amport panel. The school has served the village for generations.

Lower border

Brambles; a *deer*; *fungi*; *oak leaves*; *pheasants* and a *harvest mouse*.

Quarley Hill in winter

The church bells at Quarley

Abbotts Ann
Little Ann

ABBOTTS ANN and LITTLE ANN

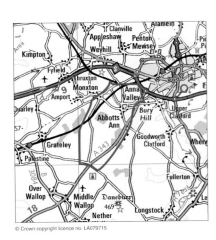

© Crown copyright licence no. LA079715

This panel is unlike any other, both in design and detail. Its designer, retired Group Captain Alan Selby, a Council colleague of Laurie Porter, lived in the village from 1951 until a year before his death in 1990. Unable to achieve the standards he sought on the proposed canvas, with 16 holes to the inch, he decided to use a finer canvas and to work the entire panel himself. Mallard Cottage and Brook Cottage, former homes of the Selbys, are depicted. Sadly, he was not to complete the mammoth task, dying after having finished almost two thirds. Happily, his daughter completed it, incorporating her own 'signature' in the panel – a whippet, in the guise of a cloud formation, to the left of the panel.

Abbotts Ann is an attractive village three miles south west of Andover. Previously 'Anna', it acquired its present name at the beginning of the tenth century when King Edward granted 15 hides of land there to the New Minster at Winchester, later to become Hyde Abbey. And 'little Anna', with five hides, was granted to the Abbey at Wherwell. Earlier, the Romans had settled there, and the remains of a villa of about AD 300 were discovered in 1854. Part of its mosaic floor is now in the British Museum.

Top border

A row of cottages at Little Ann: The cottage on the right with four dormer windows, is Mallard Cottage; *the Old Rectory*: a splendid Georgian house, now a private residence; *three Virgins' Crowns in St Mary's Church*: These represent Abbotts Ann's famous tradition of awarding a crown to any unmarried person, male or female, of unblemished character who was born, baptised and died within the parish. The crown of freshly cut hazelwood, is decorated with black and white paper rosettes. Five paper gauntlets hang from it, challenging anyone who might seek to dispute the award.

The crown is carried high in the funeral cortege by two girls dressed in white and suspended in church for three weeks. If no challenge is made it is hoisted high in the nave with a shield bearing the name and dates of the deceased. Forty-nine crowns survive, the last being awarded in 1973; *the Eagle Inn*: The present building replaced one burned down in 1865 in 'a tremendous conflagration' which destroyed many properties; *a row of cottages* in the centre of the village. The *house with the white palings* is the old School House, behind which is the school. This was built in 1831 by Robert Tasker who arrived as a blacksmith in 1806 and founded the Waterloo Ironworks.

Robert, a nonconformist, stipulated that the school should be open to children of all denominations. The school was leased by the newly-arrived Rector, the Rev. Samuel Best, who became the moving force behind its development. Fees varied with the ability of the parents to pay. More information on Taskers is given in the Upper Clatford panel description.

Middle section

The design for the middle section is a panoramic representation of the old houses of Abbotts and Little Ann from the north. The *white cottage near the T junction* (of Mill Lane with Cattle Lane) in the centre foreground is Brook Cottage. *Two buildings in Mill Lane* are of special interest, Lower Mill (featured in the Domesday Survey of 1086) and the Old Rectory. The mill, too, is now a private residence.

Opposite the Old Rectory is *St Mary's Church*. This was built in 1716 on the site of the former Saxon church by Thomas 'Diamond' Pitt, former Governor of Madras who had acquired the Manor of Abbotts Ann on his return from India in 1710. Whilst there he had bought a huge diamond of 410 carats which he sold at a vast profit to the Regent of France. The church, built in a plain style of red brick, was financed from the proceeds. In the adjacent water meadows are *six lime trees*, survivors of 12 marked on a tithe map of 1730.

The bright red building to the right of the lime trees is the *War Memorial Hall*. The first hall was a hut opened in 1920 which burned down a few years later to be replaced by a brick building which was extended in 1977 to commemorate the Queen's Silver Jubilee.

On the extreme left of the panel, by the side of the old Andover-Salisbury road, is the former *Poplar Farm*, now a restaurant. The main village road, Duck Street, is on the right with the fork to Dunkirt Lane leading into the fields. Before the Enclosure Act of 1774 the fields were sub-divided into strips cultivated by the villagers. 'Dunkirt' probably owes its origin to the nightly run of the dung cart with manure for the strips.

Lower border

This depicts the *Pillhill Brook*, formerly known as the River Anna, and some of the wild life to be seen in the water meadows. They include *woodpeckers*, *hares*, an *exotic hoopoe* and a *heron*. (There is a large heronry in the trees bordering the river in Little Ann.) A *pair of swans* nest along this stretch of water most years and *Canada geese* usually appear during the winter. In addition to various flowers, there is also a *pheasant*, a splendid *barn owl* and a *frog* squatting by the brook.

Little Ann

The Virgins' Crowns at Abbotts Ann

Upper Clatford
Goodworth Clatford
Barton Stacey
Bullington

UPPER CLATFORD, GOODWORTH CLATFORD, BARTON STACEY and BULLINGTON

© Crown copyright licence no. LA079715

The two Clatfords, Upper and Goodworth, are twin villages straddling the River Anton; although they share the same name (Clatford means 'the ford where the burdock grows'), the same school and same Rector, they are in most other respects quite different in character.

UPPER CLATFORD

Top border

Burdock leaves and flowers, symbolising the origin of the name 'Clatford'.

Middle section

In the top centre is *Bury Hill*, a 300 feet high hillfort to the west of the parish, little more than a mile from the centre of Andover. We know that some of Clatford's earliest inhabitants lived here because fragments of haematite-coated pottery found during the 1930s have been dated 6th century BC. The hill is surmounted by three lines of banks and ditches, the outer and the earliest more than half a mile long and dug to a depth of 11 feet 6 inches. The inner ditch was originally 17 feet deep while part of the excavated soil made an inner rampart 7 feet high. The construction of such a defence was a prodigious task suggesting either a powerful local leader able to command the necessary labour force or communities along the Pillhill and Anton united to create a district stronghold. The hillfort appears to have been abandoned about AD 70. Although not another 'Danebury', Bury Hill is of considerable archaeological interest.

The River Test at Upper Clatford

In the top left corner is the parish church of *All Saints*. There was a pre-Conquest church in 'Cladford' but the oldest parts of the present church probably belong to an aisleless 12th century church. In the north window of the belfry are two portions of an inscribed stone, 'Repaired in the Year of the Lord 1578'. The second north aisle and the enlargement of the chancel date from the 1890s and the vestry from 1903.

Part of the Clatfords' history is the firm of Taskers which, for more than 160 years, provided the livelihood for generations of local people. Part of the *Taskers' works* and one of their *traction engines* are depicted on the right. It all began in 1803 when Robert Tasker, a 21 year old blacksmith from near Devizes, worked in the Abbotts Ann forge. A man of vision and enterprise, Robert designed and constructed a plough which proved to be very successful. His brother joined him in 1813 and they found premises in Upper Clatford for their foundry where they made ploughs, other agricultural machinery, cast-iron pumps and domestic appliances. The business prospered and was named the Waterloo Ironworks soon after the Battle in 1815. They built workers' cottages in what became known as Waterloo Square. Their first traction engine, built in

1869, was the first steam engine to be seen on local roads.

By the end of the century various Tasker companies were making engines, threshing tackle, iron bridges and many other products. During World War I the firm made munitions and in World War II huge 'Queen Mary' low-loading trailers capable of carrying a complete fighter aircraft. Large articulated lorry trailers were manufactured here until the early 1980s. Nothing now remains of the ironworks and the site is now a housing estate. The engine in the panel is 'Little Giant', built in 1902.

The bridge with the graceful ornamental arches (lower left) is a fine example of a Tasker iron bridge which crosses the River Anton near the picturesque Fishing Cottage. In the middle centre are the *chalk pits* excavated by the Tasker brothers to provide ballast for the foundations for the works they built on Clatford Marsh. The *arched building* (bottom right corner) was a school built by the Taskers in Anna Valley in 1831. The left-hand side was home for the schoolmistress and her husband and the schoolroom was over the arch to the other side. Now known as The Lodge, it is one of the many listed buildings in the parish.

When the Lodge School was too small, the firm built another school behind the Workmen's Hall.

Lower border

King cups, clumps of which grow in Watery Lane.

Upper Clatford

Goodworth Clatford water tower

The river at Goodworth Clatford

GOODWORTH CLATFORD

Goodworth, the smaller of the two Clatfords, has also been known by the names of 'Lower' and 'Nether'. The Anglo-Saxon derivation of Goodworth is believed to be 'Goda's enclosure', but little is known of Goda.

Top border

A *'nodding donkey'*, representing the oil extraction undertaken in the parish for about two years from 1986; a *horse and rider* – there is a riding stable in the village; the *keys of St Peter* on the church crest; *crossed tennis racquets* to represent the flourishing club in the village; a *tractor*, representing farming activities.

Middle section

The *silo* in the upper right corner, a dominant local feature, which commands stunning views over the valley, was built in 1936 as a water tower and was encased in wood. To its left is the *parish church of St Peter* which, until the Dissolution of the monasteries, was a dependency of Wherwell Priory. The church began as a small nave and chancel to which a south aisle was added towards the end of the 12th century.

The 14th century saw the addition of the north aisle and the rebuilding of the tower. Both aisles were rebuilt in the 15th century. A special feature of village life in Goodworth Clatford is the sound of the eight bells in the tower (the oldest cast in 1622), which are regularly rung.

The fine *tree in the fork of the rivers*, where the Pillhill Brook joins the Anton, is a swamp cypress (Taxodium), a native of South America. On the opposite bank are several *pollarded willows*. The *swans* on the river represent the many who are permanent residents; *ducks* can also be seen lower down.

Moseley Cottage (on the right) in the centre of the village, is typical of many thatched properties. Note the *fisherman* on the bank below. The red brick building is the *Village Club*, the hub of village activities and a gift to the village from Sir Alfred Yarrow in 1923. Sir Alfred had built village clubs for two previous parishes where he had lived. He was a generous and enterprising man – and perhaps a little eccentric; he always slept in a rocking hammock as he could not settle in a fixed bed while his own burglar alarm was a device which switched all the lights on in the house simultaneously in the event of an intrusion.

The *crown and the oak tree* symbolise the Royal Oak public house. This, together with the school and Forge Cottages, was destroyed by a flying bomb on the 14th July 1944. There were deaths – refugees from London who had come to Clatford to escape the blitz! The Royal Oak, formerly on a corner site, was later rebuilt about 30 yards away.

Lower border

Burdock; a *heron*; *king cups*; *wild sorrel*; *roe deer*; *willowherb*.

BARTON STACEY AND BULLINGTON

Barton Stacey's earliest inhabitants were the Neolithic tribe who buried their dead in the long barrows, dating from 3500 to 2000 BC, on Moody Down, now the army firing range. There is evidence of a Roman camp east of Manor Farm. In Saxon times the village was Bertun ('ber' or barley and 'tun' or place), a Royal Manor of Edward the Confessor. In 1206 the Manor was bestowed on Sir Rogo de Stacey, hence the name. Barton's sister parish of Bullington lies under the shadow of Tidbury Hill with the ancient hill fort of Tidbury Ring.

Top border

The *blazing house* recalls the great fire which destroyed much of the village on 7th May 1792. A spark from the blacksmith's shop set light to some 'dry litter near a cucumber bed' which in turn ignited the thatch on the adjoining mill house. A strong wind was blowing and soon most of the houses, barns, stables, granaries and ricks were ablaze. One life was lost, that of Farmer Friend who went upstairs to rescue his fortune of 400 guineas. A contemporary report says that only a small piece of his backbone was found

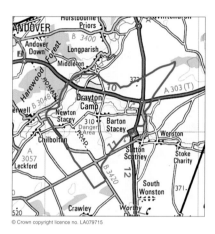

© Crown copyright licence no. LA079715

in the ashes. The fire accounts for the absence of thatched roofs in the village; the *Roman soldier* and his counterpart, the *modern soldier* in combat uniform, symbolise the fact that Army camps have been in the area from Roman to modern times. The large military camp with its many married quarters about a mile from the village centre was built just before World War II. The Allied war time leaders, Sir Winston Churchill and General Dwight Eisenhower, both visited Barton Stacey Camp in 1942 when American troops were stationed there. The camp is now a training unit for the staging of military exercises; the *corn* represents the ancient rights of villagers to thresh corn in the market place.

Swans on the Test

Middle section

The fields at the top of the panel represent those on either side of the road which climbs to Newton Stacey which is separated from Barton Stacey by a stretch of Roman road. The *red flag* flies when the Army firing range at Moody Down is in use, and *hot air balloons* and *helicopters* are a common sight. Below the cornfield a *tractor* is seen at work.

The parish church of *All Saints, Barton Stacey* is in the centre at the foot of the hill. The original church was certainly standing in the 10th century when it was known as St Victor's. During the 12th century it was rebuilt, in the Norman Transitional style. Until the run-down of Barton Stacey Camp it was the official garrison church.

Prominent in the centre is *The Swan Inn*, which is at least 200 years old. Next to it is the *village stores*, *post office* with its *red letter box*, and, most unusually for a village, a launderette. The building whose gables can be seen behind the shop is '*Homelea*', and the *group of houses* above the inn sign represent the view down the village street looking south, including 'Chestnut cottage', home of Mrs J Sambell who designed the panel. The *horse* which can just be seen at

centre right is Chammy, owned by Kim and
Claire Wainwright.

In the bottom left corner is the *viaduct*
which carried the now disused railway over
the River Dever and close to it is the
picturesque church of *St Michael and All
Angels*, Bullington which dates from the
11th century and was built by the Lord of
the Manor for the private use of his family
and workers. There are *lime trees* lining the
church path, representing the twelve apostles.
In spring the borders are carpeted with
daffodils. Above the church *a man* can be
seen *fishing* in the Dever Springs Trout
Fisheries, a commercial fishing lake.

Lower border

Deer grazing in Harewood Forest; *poppies*,
hedgehogs, and *sheep* graze in large numbers;
trout are plentiful in the Dever and anglers
can hire a rod in the trout fishery; there are
many *pheasants* and the area is a habitat for
barn owls.

Bullington church

*Norman doorway,
Bullington church*

Chilbolton
Wherwell
Longparish

Wherwell

Longparish

1988

CHILBOLTON, WHERWELL and LONGPARISH

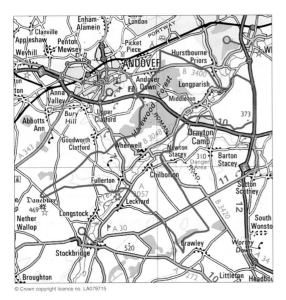

© Crown copyright licence no. LA079715

CHILBOLTON

Chilbolton is one of the largest villages in the valley of the River Test just north of its confluence with the Anton. A village of great charm, Chilbolton is a combination of picturesque thatched cottages, modern scientific developments on the old airfield site, and its common, an area with an international botanic reputation. The Test, separating it from Wherwell, forms the northern and western boundaries. Its name at the time of Domesday was Cilbodentune.

Top border

Tracery to be found on Chilbolton's pre-Reformation wafering tongs. Wafers for mid-Lent church ceremonies were baked in Chilbolton before the Normans came. The wafering tongs were used for making these unique wafers for at least three centuries. The tongs belonged to the Baverstock family who passed them, with the secret recipe, from one generation to another. The tongs, made very hot in a wood fire, produced delicately crisp and fragile wafers with ecclesiastical designs, on one side, IS for Jesus the Saviour. They were made

Chilbolton

until the 1950s and the tongs are now in Winchester Museum; *King Athelstan* who, tradition says, sought refuge in Chilbolton when harassed by the Danes around 925. It was decided to settle the ensuing seige by combat between their respective champions, Colbrand, the Danish giant, and Guy, Earl of Warwick, in a meadow outside Winchester still called Danesmead. Earl Guy was helped by a friendly crow which fluttered around the Dane, hastening his defeat. The King gave the village to the Cathedral clergy of Holy Trinity, Winchester; *'The Golden Talon'*, emblem of the 17th Airborne Division, U.S. Army. This commemorates the stay from 1944, of the division, with their troop-carrying gliders, on the airfield, living in 'Tent City'. In December of that year the gliders, packed with paratroopers, took part in the 'Battle of the Bulge' in the Belgian Ardennes. Veterans still return and in 1984 a large contingent came over for the 40th anniversary of D-Day presenting Chilbolton with an American flag which had flown on the Capitol in Washington; the *radio telescope* on West Down which can be seen for miles around. The huge dish, 80 ft across, was erected on the old airfield site in 1967 and is a steerable radio aerial operated by the Science Research Council.

Middle section

A *Spitfire* flies at the top. Chilbolton Down became an airfield, a satellite of Wallop Aerodrome, at the outbreak of World War II. Spitfires flew from here throughout the war and in 1945 thousands of Allied prisoners of war were flown into Chilbolton before their dispersal. Later, the airfield was used by the RAF for testing new jet aircraft, including the Swift and the Vampire. Most of the area was later restored to its former owners. *Fullerton Clump*, a local landmark, is depicted on the left while below is *Chilbolton Common*, declared a Site of Special Scientific Interest. It can be reached by footpath from the village or over the Test from Wherwell. It has never been ploughed or treated with chemicals and is grazed by cattle. Its banks and ditches produce both chalk tolerant and chalk hating plants, well over 100 being recorded by naturalists and scientists. It is also an important nesting site for snipe, redshank and other birds. *Purlygig Bridge* crosses a tributary of the Test. The name is thought to derive from a whirlpool (or whirlygig) under the willows on the Wherwell side of the bridge. *The village grindstone* was presented to the village by Mr Thomas Waterman, publican of the New Inn on the common, to mark the Coronation of King George V and Queen Mary. Mr Waterman was also carpenter, builder, wheelwright, undertaker and steeplejack. For years the grindstone stood under the elm tree outside the village hall and was regularly used by farmhands for sharpening scythes and sickles, but it now stands on the village green, opposite the Abbot's Mitre Inn.

Willow Cottage and *Tudor Cottage*, prominent in the panel, are typical of the attractive houses in the Conservation Area of the village. The *parish church* with the unusual dedication of St Mary-the-Less is seen behind the houses. The chancel is 13th century and the aisles 14th, and an inscription over the vestry door records that the church was restored in 1893. The south west tower and spire, constructed of stone and wood, dates from that restoration. A Lawson's Cypress, planted in the churchyard in 1897 to mark Queen Victoria's Diamond Jubilee, still stands.

Lower border

Death's Head Hawk-Moth (Acherontia atropos) seen in the village; *cowslip* (Primula veris) grows on Chilbolton Common; *lapwing* (Vanellus vanellus) nests on Chilbolton Common.

The Chilbolton Down radio aerial

WHERWELL

Wherwell on the banks of the Test, with
many thatched, timbered cottages fronting
the winding road, is claimed by many to be
one of the most attractive in the Test Valley;
it is certainly an amateur photographer's
delight. The name, 'Hwerwyl' in AD 955,
could have meant 'kettle' or 'cauldron
springs' because of its bubbling springs.
Pronunciation of the name has always been
a problem with variations ranging from
'Wher-well' through 'Wer-rel' to 'Hurrell'.

Top border

Euphemia, Abbess of Wherwell Abbey
1226-1257. She seems to have been a
medieval Florence Nightingale who,
although reputed to be sweet and pious,
'seemed to have the spirit of a man rather
than a woman'. She did much to improve
the Abbey properties. 'She also, with
maternal piety and careful forethought built,
for the use of both sick and sound, a new and
large farmery away from the main buildings
. . . Beneath the farmery she constructed a
watercourse, through which a stream flowed
with sufficient force to carry off all refuse
that might corrupt the air . . .'; a *cockatrice
monster*. Legend says that many years ago
in a dungeon beneath the priory a duck's
egg was hatched by a toad, producing a
cockatrice. When small, it was fed and cared
for. But it developed into a fearsome monster
whose hunger could only be assuaged by a
human being. Four acres of land was offered
to anyone who could slay the monster and
several people lost their lives. Then, a
servant named Green had a brilliant idea.
He lowered a huge steel mirror into the
vault and the cockatrice, seeing another of
his kind, battered himself against the mirror
for several days. When he was nearly dead
the intrepid Green went down and slew him

Wherwell

Bluebells in Harewood Forest

82

with a spear. In Harewood Forest there is still a four-acre parcel of land known as Green's Acres. A weather-vane depicting the cockatrice was formerly on the church spire but is now in Andover Museum; *Wherwell Abbey*, founded by Queen Elfrida in AD 986. Queen Matilda (Maud) 1102-1167 and King Stephen 1097-1154. *Matilda is seen fleeing from Stephen*, symbolic of the battle between their forces at Wherwell during the 15 year civil war over the succession to the throne. King Henry I made Matilda his heir. But when he died in Normandy in 1135 his nephew, Stephen de Blois, crossed to England and was crowned King in London. Matilda came to England in 1139 and joined forces with her half-brother Robert of Gloucester to contest the succession. In February 1141 Matilda's army defeated Stephen's at the Battle of Lincoln. Stephen was imprisoned in Bristol and on 3rd March, 1141 Matilda was received in state in Winchester Cathedral and elected Domina Anglorum. She proceeded to London, expecting to be crowned, but her arrogance caused a riot and she was forced to flee. Regrouping her forces, she eventually established a garrison in Wherwell Abbey. In September of that year they were defeated in a battle on the outskirts of the village by supporters of Stephen. Many were killed and others took

refuge in the abbey church which was then burned to the ground.

Intermittent fighting between Matilda and Stephen continued for several more years.

Middle section

The houses on the left of the road represent the part of the village believed to be the oldest. Some houses have wattle and daub walls. Above is the *parish church of St Peter and Holy Cross*, reached by a small bridge over the river. The church was restored in 1856-58 and fragments of the old church can be seen here and there in the village.

Above the church is the *White Lion Inn* on the hairpin bend on the road to Andover. The Priory was under siege in the Civil War but the aim of Cromwell's artillery was a little wide and two of his cannon balls are said to have dropped down the chimney of the ivy-covered 17th century inn, half a mile away. One is still on display. On the opposite side of the panel is the *old forge* which, sadly, has fallen into some decay.

Below the forge is *Wherwell Priory*, previously the home of the late Marjorie, Countess of Brecknock. The house is on

Thatched cottages at Wherwell

Church Street, Wherwell

Trout in the Test

the site of the nunnery founded by Queen Elfrida. The story is that King Edgar sent one of his courtiers, Aethelwold, to visit Elfrida, and offer marriage to the King if he considered her beauty equal to the reports. Aethelwold saw that it was and, without revealing the true object of his mission, married her himself, naively reporting that she was a girl of vulgar and commonplace appearance. Inevitably Edgar became aware of his perfidy, and invited himself to Aethelwold's manor in Harewood. The next day, while out hunting in the forest, Edgar murdered him by stabbing him in the back with a javelin. Edgar eventually married Elfrida and they had a son, Ethelred. Legend has it that after Edward's death Elfrida contrived to have Edward (the Martyr), his elder son by his former marriage, murdered at Corfe Castle so that her Ethelred (the Unready) could succeed to the throne. William of Malmesbury tells how Elfrida founded the Abbey at Wherwell, possibly as an act of penitence. The nunnery flourished until it was destroyed by Henry VIII in 1540. Nothing now remains of the Abbey but Wherwell Priory, a lovely old mansion, was built near the site.

The War Memorial with the adjacent cherry tree is depicted in the centre of the panel. The tree is no longer there, having been a casualty of the great 1987 gale. *The Test* flows beneath the bridge at the end of the road.

Lower border

Sheep; *mallard*, *swan* and *cygnet* on the Test; *pheasant*; *fallow deer* in Harewood Forest.

LONGPARISH

Longparish is a most apt name for the village as it is, indeed, a long parish, winding and twisting for three miles along the Test. The name did not appear until the middle of the 16th century, at about the time of the Dissolution of the Monasteries, before which it was known as Middleton (or Middletune).

The parish was formed from four ancient 'tithings', East and West Aston, Middleton and Forton. Apart from some postwar development of council housing, Longparish remains much as it has for centuries, with half-timbered, brick and flint cottages.

Top border

The first item refers to the *murder of Aethelwold* by King Edgar, recounted in the description of the Wherwell panel. A monument in Harewood Forest, erected in 1825 by Lt Col William Iremonger and known as Deadman's Plack, is inscribed as follows: 'About the Year of our Lord DCCCCLXIII Upon this Spot beyond Time of Memory. Called Deadman's Plack tradition reports that Edgar (Surnamed the Peaceable) King of England in the ardor of Youth Love and Indignation Slew with his own hand his treacherous and ungrateful Favourite Earl Athelwold owner of this forest of Harewood in resentment of the Earl's having basely betrayed his Royal confidence and perfidiously married his Intended Bride The beauteous Elfrida Daughter of Ordgar Earl of Devonshire, afterwards Wife to King Edward and by him mother of King Etheldred II, which Queen Elfrida after Edgar's death murdered his eldest son King Edward the Martyr and founded "The Nunnery of Wherwell"'; *Ashburn Rest* – an oak seat at a spring where, at one time, a drinking cup was fastened to the stone rim. It was erected by the Revd Burnaby-Green in 1886 for rest and refreshment of his parishioners, on their long walk to church. On it is carved, 'O ye wells, Bless ye the Lord, Praise Him and magnify him for ever'; the *stocks* are outside the churchyard wall near the east lychgate. In 1936, due to an unfortunate misunderstanding of instructions, they were replaced by stout new ones! There is no record of when they were last used; *Father Time*, the famous weather vane on the roof of Lords cricket ground, recalls the notable achievement of the Longparish Cricket Club in winning the Samuel Whitbread

Deadman's Plack monument

View towards Longparish Church

competition at Lords on 31st August 1987. Cricket at Longparish has a long history with records going back to 1878. In 1987 they played Treeton Welfare from Yorkshire, beating them by 76 runs and taking the cup home in triumph.

Middle section

The *houses* just below the skyline at the top are those at Forton at the west end of the village. The *church of St Nicholas* on the left was built between 1100 and 1200 but the chief features remaining of the original building are the nave arcades. As a memorial of the Silver Jubilee of King George V, the village subscribed to the re-hanging of the bells with one new bell to make a peal of six. In 1950 Longparish celebrated the 750th anniversary of the building of the church.

Further down the road is *the school*. This was opened in 1837 by the 'National Society for promoting the education of the poor in the principles of the Established Church'. In 1957 a new Church of England (Aided) School was built, which caters for children of primary school age from Longparish and Hurstbourne Priors with about 70 pupils. The Test flows past the boundary fence of the school site.

Opposite the church is the *village hall*, whose site was conveyed to the Diocesan Board of Finance in 1910 for the building of a church hall. In 1963 a new charity was established which leased the Longparish Village Hall to the Parish Council for a peppercorn rent, its administration being in the hands of a village management committee.

The charming *thatched cottage* below the village hall is the Old Curacy, typical of many such in the village, and below that, *The Plough public house*, one of the village's two inns. It was built during the 19th century and backs on to the Test.

Opposite is the house of *The Upper Mill* with the bridge crossing diagonally in front. This is one of two mills in the village (both mentioned in the Domesday Survey) and it is currently being restored by its owner, who has recovered three or four millstones from the river, refurbished some of the machinery and replaced some of the timber on the water wheel.

The River Test, bridged in many places and bordered by lush meadows, is a prominent feature of the village. The stretch featured in the panel, with the line of weeping willows, bullrushes, fungi and various water meadow plants, together with the bridge and the ducks, is representative of the section of the river in the village.

Lower border

Heron; *roe deer*; *mute swan*; *trout* and *kingfisher*.

Paper Mill Farm, Longparish

The river at Longparish

The Wallops
(Nether Wallop and Over Wallop)

THE WALLOPS

THE WALLOPS (NETHER WALLOP and OVER WALLOP)

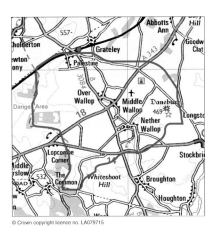

© Crown copyright licence no. LA079715

Strung along three miles of the Wallop Brook on its way to join the Test at Bossington are the three villages which take their name from the chalk stream – Nether, Middle and Over Wallop. The name derives from 'waella' (street) and 'hop' (valley) or, put more poetically, the place of springing water. Nether and Over are highly attractive villages; Middle Wallop lies between the two, clustered around the busy crossroads, and is the home of the School of Army Aviation. In The Wallops panel, Nether is on the left and Over on the right.

Army Air Corps Lynx over Middle Wallop Airfield

NETHER WALLOP

Nether Wallop follows the course of the stream for about a mile and a half, the church and village being clustered in the main bend.

Top border

Tawny owl; *pheasant*; *kingfisher*; *Paulet Coat of Arms*. It was in 1547 that Sir William Paulet, later first Marquis of Winchester, bought the Chief Manor of Nether Wallop, beginning the overlordship of the Paulet or Powlett family that was to last for 364 years; *nightingale*; *swallow*; *curlew*; *nuthatch*.

Middle section

The *helicopter* (top left) is from The School of Army Aviation based at the former RAF station built between 1938 and 1940. Throughout the war the airfield was a front line fighter station, bombed on several occasions. The Army Air Corps facility now occupies land in both Over and Nether Wallop parishes. Today it is the operational training centre for Army Aviation; its helicopter pilots overfly most villages in the district. The *airfield building* and the *red wind sock* can be seen on the left. The airfield is also the home of the Museum of

Army Flying. The School of Army Aviation, previously the Army Air Corps Centre, has the Freedom of the Borough of Test Valley 'with the right, honour and distinction of marching through the streets of the Borough on all ceremonial occasions with colours flying, bands playing, drums beating and bayonets fixed'.

At the top is *Danebury Hill Fort*, one of the finest Iron Age camps in Hampshire. Danebury Ring has acquired international archaeological importance as a result of the excavations carried out under the direction of Professor Barry Cunliffe. The largest excavation on a prehistoric site in Britain has revealed an unparalleled view of life in an Iron Age Hill Fort from about 600 BC to 50 AD. *Farming activities* are illustrated below Danebury and *two riders* are also to be seen. The building in the top right corner is *Fifehead Manor*, which legend links with Lady Godiva.

In the centre is the *parish church of St Andrew*. The original church was built about 50 years before the Norman Conquest when Nether Wallop belonged to Earl Godwin. The Normans enlarged it and built a west tower. Later, a steeple was added which lasted until 1704 when, it is recorded, 'The Tower of

Wallop Church fell down, the walls being quite rotten and decayed'. In the nave is the only known brass to an Abbess, Mary Gore, who died in 1436 and was buried in the church.

To the right of the church is the unusual 15 ft high *pyramid memorial* to Dr Francis Douce who died in 1760. He left money in his will 'that boys and girls in the parish are taught to read and write and cast an account a little way, but they must not go too far least it makes them saucy and the girls all want to be chamber maids, and in a few years you will be in want of cooks'.

The large house to the left of the church is *Garlogs* (thought to be a corruption of Gore's Lodge), the home of the aforementioned Abbess. The fact that she was buried in the church suggests that she may well have been a local girl made good. A tunnel is said to have linked the house with 'Monks' in the centre of the village. A later occupier was the brilliant jockey and trainer, Tom Cannon, great-grandfather of Lester Piggott. He developed Danebury into one of the finest stables in the country. The house with the large chimney stacks to the right of the church is the former *Wallop House*, built in 1838 on the site of the nunnery and now

View towards Danebury, with the Grandstand

Detail of mural in Nether Wallop church

St Andrew's church and Nether Wallop

Winton House Nursing Home.

In the centre foreground is *the Mill* which was in full use until 1949 not only as a mill but also as a bakery. Now it houses a fishing tackle and trout-breeding business. At the rear of the *group of cottages* on the right is the *village hall*. Running across the whole panel is the *Wallop Brook* with *willow trees* on the bank. Some of the first cricket bats were made from Wallop willows, including those used by the great Dr W G Grace. In the bottom left corner is *Place Farm* on a site probably occupied before the Conquest. Later it was the home of the Paulets, and more recently, of the celebrated conductor Leopold Stokowski.

Lower border

Flora found in the locality, including *wild arum*, *bluebells*, *dandelion clocks* and *foxglove*. Amongst the flowers is a *rabbit* and a *snail*.

OVER WALLOP

Over Wallop was described in the Domesday Book as the 'other Wallop', smaller than Nether. At the time of the Conquest it was held by King Harold, having been the home of his mother, Countess Gueda. It is here, in Townsend Field, that the Wallop Brook rises. From earliest times the main street has followed the north side of the brook, properties on the other side using plank bridges to cross.

Top border

Green woodpecker; *cuckoo*; *magpie*; *Wallop Coat of Arms*, with its heraldic 'river'. In 1208 Matthew Wallop, Warden of Winchester, was granted land in the village. One of the panels of the 15th century font bears the crest of the family. One branch became Earls of Portsmouth who owned the greater part of Over Wallop for four centuries; *green plover*; *barn owl*.

Middle section

The background at the top represents farming activities, with *grazing sheep*, a *tractor* ploughing and a *cornfield*.

The house in the top left corner is *Blacksmiths Farm*. This was built in the early 18th century of brick and flint, an annexe being added in 1852. The timber-framed and thatched cottage in the centre is *South View*, with wattle and daub walls dating from about 1540. The small rectangle in the roof is reputed to be the smugglers' window, from which the excise men could be seen approaching. Next to it is the *White Hart Inn*, an early 18th century coaching inn. Beer was brewed there and evidence of the vats can be seen in the cellars.

On 16 February 1982 the roof was destroyed by fire. During the conflagration one or two regulars were loath to leave the bar!

On the left in the next row is *Forresters*, an elegant Queen Anne house, the home for several generations of the Clarke family who were local builders. The two buildings on the other side of the War memorial are the *Church Farm barn and house*, home to generations of the Shadwell family. The 18th century barn has both chalk cob and boarded walls and a thatched roof. It is still in use. In front can be seen three of the family's herd of *Guernsey cows* which twice a day make their slow 200 yard trek between grazing and milking. Until 1992 the family

ran its own milk round. Some wheat grown on the farm's 100 acres is for thatching.

The *War Memorial Cross* in the centre of the panel, listing the 19 from the village who had fallen in the war, was unveiled in October 1919. Glider Pilot Regiment veterans regularly attend Remembrance Day services. In the bottom left corner is *King's Farm*. This attractive early Georgian house at the foot of Orange Lane is brick built, partly timber framed and bears the date 1738. Orange Lane is so called because tradition has it that Wallop had the honour of accommodating William of Orange and his army en route from Brixham to London but recent research indicates that his progress was well to the west of the village. It could well, however, have had repercussions in the village.

In the centre at the bottom is *St Peter's Church Hall*. Built in 1853 (for £255) it served as the Church School until 1895 when the Council School was opened.

St Peter's Church occupies the bottom right corner. It underwent a major restoration in 1866 under the supervision of J L Pearson, architect to Truro Cathedral, but the 15th century octagonal font and the 13th century

piscina were retained. The 'saddleback' bell tower houses five bells, the oldest dated 1631.

Lower border

This continues the Nether Wallop theme of *wild flowers* found locally, with a hovering *damsel fly*.

The Wallop Brook

Stockbridge
Longstock
Leckford

The BOROUGH of TEST VALLEY

DEC·TESTE·VALEANW

Linkenholt
Vernham Faccombe
Dean
Hurstbourne Tarrant
Tangley
Fyfield Smannell
Appleshaw Charlton
Kimpton Penton Grafton
Thruxton Andover
Penton Mewsey
South Tedworth
Amport Longparish
Shipton Bellinger Monxton Upper Clatford
Quarley Abbotts Ann Goodworth Clatford
Grateley Bullington
Wherwell Barton Stacey
Over Wallop Longstock Chilbolton
Nether Wallop Leckford
Stockbridge
Broughton Houghton Little Somborne
Buckholt
Bossington
West Tytherley Ashley
Kings Somborne
East Tytherley
Frenchmoor
Mottisfont Braishfield
East Dean
Lockerley Michelmersh
Sherfield English Awbridge Ampfield
Melchet Park Romsey
Plaitford North Baddesley
Wellow
Chilworth
Nursling
Rownhams

I chatter, chatter, as I flow
To join the brimming river,
For men may come and men may go,
But I go on for ever.

from Tennyson's 'The Brook'
quoted by Lord Denning at
the first public exhibition
June 1990

Robina Orchard

STOCKBRIDGE
LONGSTOCK
LECKFORD

STOCKBRIDGE, LONGSTOCK and LECKFORD

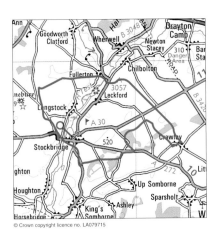

© Crown copyright licence no. LA079715

The decision to include a map of the Borough was taken during discussions on what should fill the space next to the Stockbridge, Longstock and Leckford section.

The verse, from 'The Brook' by Alfred, Lord Tennyson, was quoted by Lord Denning at the first public showing of the panels in Andover Museum in July 1990.

STOCKBRIDGE

On a causeway of compressed chalk laid down in the remote past for a crossing of the River Test, Stockbridge is almost midway between Andover to the north and Romsey to the south. There have been settlements on Stockbridge Down since at least the second millennium BC; within a short distance are the impressive earthworks at Danebury, Meon Hill and Woolbury. Two ancient roads meet and cross at Stockbridge, one running east to west between Winchester and Old Sarum, later Salisbury, and the other running north and south along the valley of the Test. The prosperity of Stockbridge has always stemmed largely from the roads which pass through it.

The 'town' (actually little more than a single row of buildings on each side of the wide main street) grew in importance when Welsh drovers rested there with their flocks on their way to various sheep fairs and markets. A thatched cottage known as 'Drovers House' has the message in Welsh painted on the wall: 'Seasoned hay, tasty pastures, good beer, comfortable beds'.

Top border

A peat spade. For centuries peat was dug in the valley, notably at Longstock and Stockbridge. Tradition has it that farmers would grant their labourers an annual day off work to cut peat and allow them the use of a farm cart to carry it home; a *Danish ship*: this is a reminder of the days when the Test was navigable and Danish invaders are thought to have dug a wide channel in the water meadows at Longstock for their flat bottomed boats. The channel was about 300 feet long and the excavated earth was piled up to form a primitive quay. The 'dock' probably served both as a base for further exploration and for the despatch of looted goods; *an eel trap, fishing flies, trout and net*: the Test, 'the queen of chalk streams', has served the angler well. Many claim it to be the finest trout stream in the world. The artificial flies are typical of the very realistic and intriguingly named creations tied so lovingly by enthusiasts.

The Stockbridge Silver Mace is part of the regalia of ancient Court Leets and Baron: The Courts are a survival of a system of jurisdiction of the Middle Ages for the settlement of local disputes, the maintenance of common pastures and ditches and the punishment of minor offences.

The Lord of the manor presided over the annual courts whose officers were a Bailiff, a Constable (now called Sergeant-at-Mace) and Hayward. From 1563 to 1832 Stockbridge was a Borough with the right to return two Members to Parliament. The Bailiff organised the voting system which was subject to considerable corruption. The Mace and Seal both having been given to the Borough as bribes, are evidence of such corruption. The Mace came from an aspiring candidate, Essex Strode, in 1681 and bore the arms of the sovereign and the donor together with an inscription (in Latin): 'Here I am, a glory to Stockbridge, by the gift of Essex Strode.' In spite of his bribe, Strode was defeated by an opponent who paid cash. Stockbridge kept the Mace! The Courts were in abeyance for almost 30 years from 1891 when Hicks Lancashire pawned the manor to recoup losses incurred over a court case which had been taken to the House of Lords by the inhabitants of Stockbridge when he attempted to appropriate the Common Down. Fortunately the mace, seal and Hayward's staff were retained by the steward of the manor who knew that they did not belong to Lancashire.

In 1920 they were handed over to Norman Hill, a Liverpool solicitor who had retired

The main street of Stockbridge

Stokes' Garage

to Stockbridge. In 1921 he reinstated the ceremony of the Courts. After his death in 1944 the manor passed to his daughter, historian Professor Rosalind Hill, and in March 1994 there were great celebrations at Stockbridge to mark the 50th anniversary of her unique service as Quondam Lady of the Manor. The National Trust now holds the Lordship.

Middle section

At the top on the left is the *parish church of St Nicholas, Leckford* and its lychgate. The church, with flint walls and small weather-board bell turret, dates from the 15th century, but the chancel was rebuilt early in the 16th century out of alignment with the nave, probably to allow space for processions between the church and the churchyard boundary. Much of the village is owned by the John Lewis Partnership whose Water Gardens at Longstock are a spectacular feature and are open to the public on one Sunday each month in the summer. Below the church is the *Peat Spade public house* and the *parish church of St Mary, Longstock*, with its lychgate. The church is comparatively modern (1876/1880) but designed in the style of the 13th century. The tower contains five bells.

In front of the church is an example of the *thatched fishing huts* which are an attractive feature of this stretch of the river. On the opposite bank is an *angler* who seems to have made a catch.

To the top right is the *chancel of the old chapel of St Peter*, dating from the 12th century. All but the nave was demolished in 1866 and it gradually fell into disrepair. In 1963, however, it was re-hallowed and since then has been extensively refurbished. Below is the *parish church of St Peter*, built in the 1860s.

To the left of old St Peter's Church is the distinctive *Town Hall*, built about 1810 at his own expense by John Foster Barham who represented the Borough for many years in Parliament. By 1820 he owned at least 80 houses in Stockbridge, but following a financial setback in 1822, sold 72 of his houses to his political opponent, Lord Grosvenor, and applied for the Chiltern Hundreds. Note the *two red telephone kiosks* near the Town Hall. When the panel was worked their days were thought to be numbered but they are still there!

Lord Grosvenor's name is perpetuated by the *Grosvenor Hotel*, an attractive building with the large porch and upper room supported on slender columns. The old market hall is incorporated into the hotel. The room above the porch is the private sanctum of the Houghton Fishing Club, the most prestigious club for dry-fly fishermen in the country, founded in 1822. The Houghton Club is limited to 17 members and records are kept of every fish taken and the fly used.

Race horses can just be seen on the sky line above the Town Hall. Racing was held for decades on a racecourse below Danebury from where the remains of the grandstand can still be seen. King Edward VII, when Prince of Wales, was a regular visitor, delighting boys by throwing pennies to them from his carriage.

Lower border

The flora and fauna of the Test Valley: *cows*; *dragonflies*; *ducks*; a *trout*; a really splendid *cockerel*.

Eel traps at Longstock

Longstock village

Houghton
Bossington
Broughton

HOUGHTON, BOSSINGTON and BROUGHTON

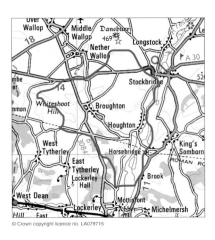

© Crown copyright licence no. LA079715

Houghton gives its name to the exclusive fishing club whose headquarters are in Stockbridge but whose stretch of the Test flows through the parish. Broughton, with its many timbered and flower-bedecked thatched cottages, two miles away on the Wallop Brook, is one of the largest villages in Test Valley. In between is Bossington House whose owner in 1829 destroyed the surrounding hamlet.

HOUGHTON AND BOSSINGTON

Top border

A *game keeper and his dog*, representing local shooting interests; a *barge* loaded with locally cut chalk blocks which would have been transported along the Redbridge to Andover canal (Mendip lead, bearing the name of the Emperor Nero and dated AD 59, was unearthed at Bossington in 1783 during excavations for the canal); *Henry V's army* under the Earl of Huntingdon camped at Bossington before leaving for France and the Battle of Agincourt in 1415. Henry is said to have attended the church at Bossington and a local field is still called Agincourt; a *wool merchant* loading his mule and a *sheep shearer*. Sheep were driven through Houghton on their way to sheep fairs in Stockbridge and Weyhill; a *soldier*, representing those who served in both world wars; a *Roman centurion*. The Roman road from Winchester to Sarum passed close by.

The river at Houghton Mill

Middle section

Houghton's 12th century *All Saints Church* is in the centre. Unusually, there are 3 arched arcades in the south aisle but only 2 in the north. On some columns can be seen medieval crosses carved by pilgrims on their way to St Swithun's shrine at Winchester. To the left of the church is the *sheepbridge* arching over the river with the poplar trees beyond and part of *Houghton Lodge*, built by the river about 1800 and now noted for its magnificent display of daffodils at Easter. Above the church roof is *Bossington House*, with its cedar tree, home of John Fairey of the aviation family. He flies his *Fairey Flycatcher* over the house. *Hereford cattle* graze below the bridge and nearby a *badger* can be seen. In the left foreground is the *Boot Inn*, and beyond are *Wayside Cottages*, originally built for the Inn's ostlers. To the right is the well-known *wheelright's workshop* in front of which is a *thatcher*, with his straw bundles, about to work on one of the cottages. A *fisherman* wades in the river while a *swan* floats gracefully by the *willow tree*. A *kestrel* hovers and *mallards* are on the wing above *Houghton Lodge*.

Lower border

The *bullrush, yellow mimulus, water avens, moorhen, water rail* and *orange balsam* represent the wildlife of the river and water meadows as do the *trout, grey wagtail, kingfisher, marsh marigold, shrew* and *barn owl*. The *hare, tiger moth, wild strawberry, field bindweed, red squirrel, orange tip butterfly, rosebay willowherb* and *ragged robin* are all to be found in the surrounding countryside.

John Fairey with a replica Fairey Flycatcher

Bossington Church

BROUGHTON

Top border

To the right of the centurion, the shepherd represents the ancient sheep drove which passed through Broughton on its way to the Stockbridge and Weyhill sheep fairs: the *juggler*, the *girl carrying produce*, the *stall*, the *King* and the *goosegirl* all represent the granting by Henry III in 1248 of a weekly market at the Manor of Broughton and a yearly fair on the feast of St Mary Magdalene; the next figures are *William Steele and his daughter Anne*. In 1699 William Steele was ordained Baptist Pastor. Anne wrote 144 hymns, 34 psalms and about 50 poems; *two boys* stand in front of the school endowed in 1601 by Thomas Dowse, Lord of the Manor of Broughton, for a schoolmaster to teach children to read, write and understand arithmetic. The charity is still administered by the Rector and trustees; a *village black-smith*. Once there were six blacksmiths in Broughton; above him is the *sign of the greyhound*, now used by one of the public houses and originally part of the arms of Thomas Dowse.

Middle section

In the centre is the *dovecote* or columbarium in the graveyard of the church. The present structure was built in 1684 on the site of one built in 1340. There are 482 'L'-shaped nesting boxes in the thickness of the walls. The oldest part of the parish *church of St Mary the Virgin* dates from the 12th century. About 1220 the nave was lengthened and the present west door built, while the tower was added in the fifteenth century. In the churchyard are ancient *Irish yews*. The *church clock* is set at eight o'clock, a reminder that until 1963 a curfew bell was rung daily at 8pm from Michaelmas Day to Lady Day to tell householders to douse their fires to minimise the risk to thatched roofs.

In the centre right of the main section is the *Baptist Chapel* which dates from 1816 with a reminder on the stone on the front of the building that the Baptist faith was established in Broughton in 1655. The pews were made from timbers from HMS 'The Royal George'. The *houses* between the Baptist Church and the Dovecote are modern village homes, whilst that between the dovecote and the parish church represents the many *thatched cottages*. In the background is *Broughton Down*, with the chalk track up to Whiteshoot

Broughton dovecote

Hill on the right. Below this are *fields* of hay, corn and grazing cattle and horses, all part of village farming. Just visible at the top right of the Baptist Church is the village *community bus* which, with volunteer drivers, operates regular services to Romsey, Salisbury, Winchester and Southampton.

The *deer*, *heron*, *wild duck*, *swans* and *willow trees* are all seen on or near the Wallop Brook as it flows through the village to join the Test at Bossington. The two *horseriders* near the bridge and the *pheasants* in the foreground represent sporting pursuits, while the Hampshire Down *sheep* in the corner are another indication of the agricultural nature of Broughton.

Lower border

The *barn owl* in flight (shared with the Houghton section), *mallard*, *flag iris* and *water crowfoot* are all found in the Wallop Brook and adjacent water meadows. The *harebell*, *spotted woodpecker*, *stoat*, *dog rose*, *rabbit*, *lapwing* and *fox* live in the surrounding countryside. The *chalk blue butterfly* feeding on *horseshoe vetch*, the *orchid* and the *cowslip* are denizens of Broughton Down while the *ears of wheat*, the *mayweed* and the *poppy* represent the arable fields.

View over Broughton and the Wallop Brook

King's Somborne
Little Somborne
Up Somborne
Ashley

KING'S SOMBORNE, LITTLE SOMBORNE, UP SOMBORNE and ASHLEY

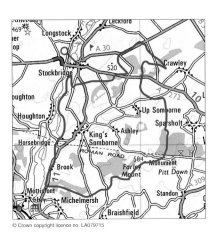

© Crown copyright licence no. LA079715

The 'Sombornes' comprise the scattered village of King's Somborne, with its centre clustered attractively around the parish church and the village green, together with the hamlets of Up Somborne, Ashley and Eldon. Up Somborne, three miles from the village itself, has a cherished gem of a church of Saxon origin now redundant but restored. Ashley, the 'gateway' to Farley Mount has its own redundant church as has lonely Eldon, once the smallest parish in England, with yet a third redundant church in a lawn in front of a farm house. The parish of Somborne with Ashley must surely be the only one in the United Kingdom with three restored, redundant churches.

Flowing through the village is the Somborne stream which rises beyond Up Somborne towards the Rack and Manger public house on the A272 and joins the Test at Horsebridge. Normally a well behaved, short-lived bourne, it flooded extensively in the spring of 1994 and far worse yet again in 1995 causing much distress and the evacuation of several cottages.

Archaeological excavations during the 1980s in the churchyard, Old Palace Farm and on the school site suggests that there was an important Saxon settlement in the area. At the time of Domesday, Somborne was part of the royal demesne.

John of Gaunt, fourth son of King Edward III, inherited the manor through his first wife, Blanche, daughter of the first Duke of Lancaster. Their son, Henry of Bolingbroke, became King Henry IV in 1399. The banks of the John of Gaunt Deer Park can still be traced between the village and the River Test but there is little evidence for the attractive notion that he resided here for any length of time or hunted in his park.

The village achieved renown through the Vicar, the Revd Richard Dawes, later Dean of Hereford, who, in 1842, founded the village school which, owing to his visionary educational philosophy, was widely regarded as a model of its kind.

Top border

A Crusader with shield and banner, the *crest of the Hervey-Bathurst family* of Somborne Park; *a motte and bailey castle* built about 1100 at Ashley, then part of the Royal Forest of Bere; a *Roman centurion*: the Roman road from Winchester to Old Sarum passed through the parish; the *monument at Farley Mount*, actually a few yards outside the Test Valley Borough Boundary, was erected on top of a Bronze Age burial mound as a memorial to a horse, later known as 'Beware Chalk Pit', which survived with its rider after jumping into a 25 feet-deep chalk pit. The next year it went on to win the 1734 Hunters Cup at Worthy Down. The horse is buried under the monument; a German *Junkers 88* bomber was shot down in the village by a Spitfire on 21 September 1940, during the Battle of Britain, the crew of four being killed. In 1951 a memorial stone to them was erected a few yards outside the Test Valley Borough boundary, at Hoplands, incorrectly recording the date as 23 September; *the brasses* (c1380) in the chancel of the church, traditionally thought to be of John of Gaunt's stewards, father and son; the *Revd Richard Dawes*, Vicar 1836-1850 who founded the village school: *John of Gaunt's archery butt*, the protected mound of which is still in a local garden; representation of *local organisations* including uniformed groups and the WI; the *'Sprat and Winkle' line*: which opened in 1865, running from Southampton to Andover along the line of the old canal. Somborne was served by Horsebridge Station but the line closed in September 1964; *John of Gaunt*, born in 1340 the third son of King Edward III; the *crest of Sir Thomas Sopwith*, the aviation pioneer, who lived at Compton Manor for more than 40 years and died there in 1989 at the age of 101; a World War I *Sopwith Camel* and his *yacht 'Endeavour'* in which he competed for the Americas' Cup.

Little Somborne Church

Middle section

Prominent in the centre of the panel, thanks to the generosity of Herbert Johnson of Marsh Court, is the elegant *War Memorial* designed by Lutyens. Behind it is the *parish church of St Peter and St Paul* largely the result of a major Victorian restoration in 1885 but a section of the south arcades of the nave dates from about 1240. The font is, however, Norman, the only relic of the earlier church.

To the right of the church is the Revd Richard Dawes' *school* of 1842. His ideas were in some ways almost a century ahead of his times both educationally and socially. The school soon acquired national recognition and Dawes was encouraged to write extensively about it, his pamphlets having a great influence on 19th century educational thought and practice.

To the left of the church is the 18th century thatched *Crown Inn* and the adjacent *Crown Cottage* with fine topiary work. Above the War Memorial is the 15th century *Cruck Cottage*, a typical two-bay cruck, the three 'cruck' tresses of naturally bent oak trees forming the framework for two rooms and supporting the roof. Between Cruck Cottage and the tower of the church is a field of *oil-seed rape*, a fairly new farming feature when the panel was worked.

In the bottom left hand corner is *Marsh Court*. This remarkable house was built of chalk by Sir Edwin Lutyens for financier Herbert Johnson, between 1901 and 1904. Gertrude Jeckyll designed the gardens. In 1926 the ballroom, also designed by Lutyens, was added. For more than forty years, until 1989, Marsh Court housed a prep school but in 1993 it was purchased for massive

refurbishment as a family home for an MP. Above Marsh Court is the restored gem of a *Saxon Church* at Little Somborne, and *Somborne Park*, seat of the Hervey-Bathursts. The church was declared redundant in 1974 and was fully restored by the Redundant Churches Fund in 1976-77, when archaeologists recorded in detail every part of the structure. Sir Thomas and Lady Sopwith are buried in the churchyard.

Up Somborne, a small farming village, is in the top left hand corner of the panel. A *combine harvester* is at work in a cornfield and a *tractor* ploughing in another. To the right of Up Somborne is *Ashley* with the little *church of St Mary*. This was also declared redundant in 1976 and subsequently extensively restored. The fine specimen *yew tree* was blown down in the great gale. The thatched *ancient well*, long a picturesque feature, was burned down by vandals in 1991 but restored with a tiled roof by the people of Ashley in 1993. To the right of the church is *Ashley Manor*. The pool in front of the house is one of a series of pools and pens which house the unique Ashley Waterfowl Collection of rare and endangered species. The *thatched cottage* is 'Little Thatches' which also has internal cruck beams. The *memorial on Farley Mount* can just be seen on the skyline. To the right of Ashley is *Hoplands*, an equestrian area, and, below it, the retirement cottages in *Humber View*. The small farming hamlet of *Eldon* is seen in the top right hand corner. The small, redundant chapel is in the farm complex. Eldon is now well-known for its rare breed of pigs and sausage manufacture.

Flying over *Compton Manor*, the former home of the late Sir Thomas Sopwith, is a *red Wessex helicopter* of the Queen's Flight used by Prince Charles who, with other members of the Royal Family, often enjoyed the excellent shooting on the estate. The *chalk pits* at Brook are a local landmark. In the lower right hand corner is *Horsebridge Mill*, one of three mentioned in the Domesday Survey, now used for the manufacture of scientific measuring instruments. Behind the mill is part of *John of Gaunt's deer park*.

Two long distance footpaths, the Test Way along the old railway, and the Clarendon Way from Winchester to Salisbury, cross in the village. The *walkers* in the bottom left hand corner represent the many ramblers who pass through the village. At the other side of the panel the late *Mike Simms* is seen fishing in the John of Gaunt lake which he established. Two *local children* by the stream

watch the swans while Ian Wilson's *bull terrie*r, Puckeridge, waits patiently.

Lower border

Increasingly rare *barn owls*; *snowdrop* and *poppy*; *butterflies* including the rare Chalk Blue; *kingfisher* and *heron*; *lilies of the valley*, *pheasants*; the *parish names*, *panel date* and *fruit*; *pedigree cow and bull*; *cowslips*; *foxes*; the rare *green fritillary*; *sheep*, *pig* and *deer*; rare varieties of *orchid*.

Horsebridge Mill

Horsebridge Station

**Mottisfont
Nursling and Rownhams
East Tytherley**

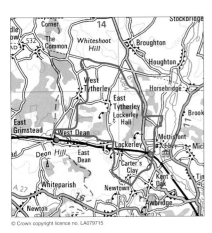

© Crown copyright licence no. LA079715

Mottisfont Abbey

MOTTISFONT

Mottisfont would not be of such interest were it not for the magnificent Abbey, built in the water meadows by the River Test, around which the village grew up.

Top border

The *bears and ragged staff* in the centre represent the coat of arms of the Barker-Mills family which acquired the Abbey House in 1684. Stone chained bears are mounted on the gate piers to both entrances; the *tiles on either side* show the 13th century tiles from the floor of the Priory, found in rubble in nearby fields. A number were built into the Abbey summerhouse during the 18th century.

Middle section

At the centre is *Mottisfont Abbey* which is surrounded by magnificent grounds with spacious lawns and mammoth plane, cedar, chestnut and beech trees. In the garden is a crystal clear spring which flows at 200 gallons a minute to join the Test, and an ice house, one of two in the village.

The Priory of Holy Trinity was established in 1201 by William Briwere, an officer of Richard I.

It was suppressed at the Dissolution and in 1536 was given by Henry VIII to Lord Sandys, his Lord Chamberlain, in return for the villages of Chelsea and Paddington! He adapted it for domestic use, siting the main rooms in the nave. The 'new' façade was built for Sir Richard Mill in 1743.

Until 1934 the Abbey remained in the ownership of Lord Sandys' family, albeit with several changes of name. In 1934 it was bought by Gilbert Russell on whose death in 1957 the house passed to the National Trust.

The *parish church of St Andrew* dates in part from the first half of the 12th Century, the chancel being extended three centuries later. It houses a rare 17th century clock movement.

In the top right corner is the *Post Office*, for many years the village stores, which is now renowned for its cream teas. In the top left corner is the *Mill Arms* at Dunbridge, once a coaching inn. The long, low white extension is now a popular skittle alley.

Below the Abbey is a beautiful stretch of the Test and in the foreground the famous *Mottisfont or Oakley Oak* tree which is probably more than a thousand years old. It is now hollow and cows have often calved inside it.

Lower border

The *roses* on either side represent the rose garden laid out in 1972 by Graham Stuart Thomas as a show place for the National Trust's collection of historic roses which he had gathered during his long career as its Garden Adviser. There are now more than 340 named varieties in the collection. In between are some of the fauna and flora which abound in and around the village: the *deer, Canada geese, swans, primroses, Speckled Wood butterfly* and a *barn owl*.

NURSLING and ROWNHAMS

The ancient settlement of Nursling, formerly Nutshalling ('the nut grove by the water meadows') now with a post-war shopping centre, housing estates, hall and school, is divided by the M27 motorway from the Victorian village of Rownhams, also extended by substantial post-war development.

Top border

In the centre is *St. Boniface*, named 'Winfrith' when he was born in Crediton in 680. After studying at the Benedictine Abbey at Exeter he became Abbott of the monastery at Nursling in 717. Two years later as Boniface he was given a Papal commission to conduct an evangelical mission to what is now Germany. In 754 he and fifty of his followers were murdered by a heathen mob; the *two crests* are those of the *Barker-Mills family* (left), and the *Mountbatten family*, both large land-owners in the area.

Middle section

The mock-gothic *parish church of St John*, Rownhams, is on the left. This was built in 1856 for the new parish created from parts of Nursling and Chilworth.

The River Test at Mottisfont

Mottisfont Abbey gardens

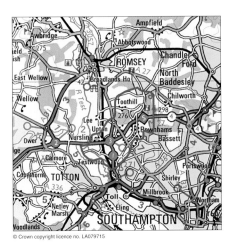

Rownhams House (top right) is the only surviving example of many large middle-class residences built for Southampton businesssmen in the second half of the 18th century. Below it is *Ivy Cottage*, one of the oldest houses in the area, probably dating from the 16th century. Between it and the church is the *radio mast* erected on top of an underground reservoir at Toothill. The line below the church and Ivy Cottage represents the M27.

The popular *Romsey Golf Course* is shown on the left and to its right is *Grove Place*, a splendid Elizabethan mansion built for John Paget between 1565 and 1585. At one time it served as a lunatic asylum, and in World War II it was an American base. In 1961 it was converted into a boys' boarding school named Northcliffe School.

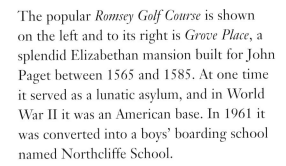

© Crown copyright licence no. LA079715

In the bottom right corner is *St Boniface Church*, Nursling, an early 14th century decorated style country church with evidence of an earlier, possibly Saxon, building. To its left is the only surviving *mill* in Nursling. A plaque on the wall records that it was built in 1728 on a frame of large beech timbers given by Sir Richard Mill. Behind it is a *pylon*, one of many which dominate the skyline. The *phragmites reed* and the *spotted*

orchid are examples of plants in the Lower Test Reserve, established in 1978.

Lower border

An *oak branch*, symbolising the sacred oak of pagan German tribes which, according to legend, was chopped down by Boniface; a *salmon*; *hazel nuts*, a reference to the name Nutshalling; a *green woodpecker*, once common but becoming rarer.

Nursling

116

EAST TYTHERLEY

East Tytherley is the smallest village in Test Valley and one of the smallest in Hampshire. Its old English name suggests that it was a 'little place with water and pasturage', a description which still holds good. In 1335 Edward III gave Tytherley to Queen Philippa who sought refuge there with her court when London was afflicted with the plague. Sadly, two of her courtiers were already infected and soon they and three-quarters of the villagers had died.

Top border

The *five butterflies* were described at the time as 'local' but sadly the designer of the panel has since died and neither her notes nor her drawings survive. A local naturalist is unable to identify the first, which appears to be a moth, but suggests that, allowing for some artistic licence, the other four could be: small tortoiseshell; swallowtail; orange tip; small copper.

Middle section

The *parish church of St Peter* replaced an earlier building in the middle of the 13th century, and remained almost unaltered until 1863 when the porch, transept and vestry were added. Thirty years later the tower was built. The giant *yew tree* was planted by Denys Rolle, Lord of the Manor from 1755.

Behind the church is a field of *oil-seed rape*. Next to the church is the attractive timbered *Letterbox Cottage* with its comparatively rare Victorian letter box. Above it hovers a *kestrel*, one of several birds of prey which nest locally. The Manor was acquired by Sir Francis Rolle in 1672. *Rolle House*, below Letterbox Cottage, was established in 1718 by Sarah Rolle as a charity school, one of the earliest in England, 'for four poor boys and six poor girls. . . to be decently clothed in blue . . . to have a halfpenny loaf of brown bread and a halfpenny worth of cheese every day that they should come to school . . . .' Her charity still benefits local children. Rolle House is now a private residence. On the right is the stump of a *tulip tree* partially blown down in the 1987 gale.

The *Star Inn* is splendidly represented in the bottom left corner. Within living memory one of two shops in the village was located in The Star. Although neither shop survives, the skittle alley in the pub is a popular rendezvous. The *sheep* in the park and the *cows* in the foreground represent local farming activities.

Lower border

The *village name* and a charming little *mouse*.

Sheep in Tytherley Park

Michelmersh
Braishfield
Lockerley

MESOLITHIC MAN   ROMAN VILLA   NAPOLEONIC WARS   SPANISH ARMADA

BROOM HILL   FERN HILL   FARLEY-DOWN

MICHELMERSH

BRAISHFIELD

LOCKERLEY

MICHELMERSH, BRAISHFIELD and LOCKERLEY

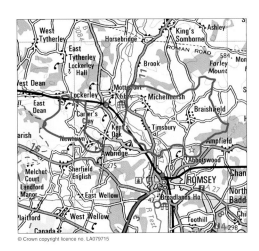

© Crown copyright licence no. LA079715

Michelmersh Church

MICHELMERSH

Michelmersh is a scattered village spread out on high ground which drops down to the Test on the far side of the A3057 Stockbridge to Romsey Road. In 985 King Athelred granted the village its charter, the millenium of which was celebrated enthusiastically in 1985.

Top border

Queen Emma, who presented the Manor of Michelmersh to St. Swithun at Winchester in 1043. On the table beside her is the Michelmersh Pot, a late Saxon pot found intact inside a small kiln discovered in a garden at Haccups Point in the late 1970s; the *archer and mounted knight* refer to the tradition that in 1415 more than six hundred knights and archers camped in the parish before setting sail for France and the Battle of Agincourt. The field is still known as Agincourt Field; the *gentleman on the black horse* is Sir William Ogle who defended Winchester Castle for the King against Cromwell in 1645. His second wife Sarah, owned Manor Farm in Michelmersh. Legend has it that his ghostly carriage is heard in the lanes at night; the *soldier on sentry duty* and the *army truck* represent the

units, including Canadian forces, which camped here before the D-day invasion of Normandy; the *bricks* are those still made from local clay.

Middle section

In the centre at the top is the *parish church* dedicated to 'Our Lady' but known as St Mary's. It is 13th century, probably built on Saxon foundations. Its unusual wooden bell-tower was added in the 15th century. One of the memorials is a cross-legged effigy of a Crusader knight with a stag at his feet. There is also one of Sir William Ogle. To the left is *the barn*, formerly an unusual five-bayed granary, now refurbished and the venue for village activities. Part of the film 'Worzel Gummidge' was made there. *The fields* show local arable farming. Top right is *Michelmersh Court*, which was formerly the Rectory when Michelmersh was one of the richest livings in the country. It is now the family home of Sir David Frost.

The house on the left below the barn is the *Old House*, formerly the Dower House, home of Sir William Ogle and is said to be the destination for his ghost! The yellow bricked house is *Michelmersh House*, originally Michelmersh Farm House and below the *sheep* is *Manor Farm*, the site associated with Queen Emma's gift to Winchester, probably the oldest building in the village.

In the left centre, below the Old House, are *strawberries* at Yew Tree Farm which, with other fruit and vegetables, has long been a popular 'pick-your-own' venue. The *row of cottages* to the right of the strawberry field are houses built for estate workers during the last century. Most have been modernised and extended including the one occupied by Shirley Morrish, the panel's designer. The fine house on the right is *The Old Rectory*. Below the strawberry field is one of the *postwar houses*. To the left of the *red telephone kiosk* is the *Old Bakery* where villagers took their cakes to be cooked. Below the bakery is a *small bungalow*, typical of a number built in the 1930s. At the other side is the *smithy*, happily still functioning with Les Ninnim wielding the hammer and tongs.

In the centre is the *Michelmersh Brick Company*, Britain's largest manufacturer of traditional handmade bricks and roofing tiles. Michelmersh craftsmen have been making bricks with the abundant clay for at least a thousand years. Michelmersh bricks are used in prestigious new buildings and the refurbishment of stately homes all over the country.

The bottom corner features a *stretch of the River Test* which forms the western boundary of the parish, and *cattle* which symbolise local dairy farming. Opposite is the *Bear and Ragged Staff*, the village public house. The signboard bears the coat of arms of the Earls of Warwick because the first Earl was known as the 'Bear' having strangled one single-handed, whilst another is reputed to have slain a giant with a tree-shaped club, hence 'The Bear and Ragged Staff'. At one time it was celebrated for cock fighting but now is renowned for an annual pumpkin competition. In front of the pub is the *Michelmersh Silver Band* which celebrated its centenary in 1985. It was originally formed as a Temperance Band and at least one village family has had an unbroken relationship with it since its formation.

Lower border

A *willow tree*; two *swallows* and a *swan* found in the lower part of the village; the *village name* surrounded by some of the flowers which grow there. The right hand side has a *barn owl*, a *deer* and an *oak tree* for the higher part of the village.

A laid hedge at Timsbury

Michelmersh brickworks

BRAISHFIELD

Braishfield, formerly part of Michelmersh, is not mentioned in the Domesday Book, but the parish contains a number of prehistoric settlement sites and a probable Roman villa. The present straggling village is a tasteful combination of old and new.

Top border

Mesolithic Man. Excavations were started on Broom Hill in 1971 by Michael O'Malley, a keen archaeologist who spent several summers working alone on the isolated hilltop. He surveyed what was described as 'a combination of an Iron Age round house with an Anglo Saxon sunken hut', and recovered over 89,000 worked flints, the largest Later Mesolithic find from a British site; a separate excavation on nearby *Fern Hill* carried out by volunteers of the Lower Test Valley Archaeological Study Group under the direction of Kevin Stubbs from 1975 to 1979 uncovered the remains of a Roman bath house, apparently built in the late third or early 4th century AD; the *oak tree*, the village emblem, stands in the school grounds; the *red coat soldier* and the flags represent the semaphore station known to have been one of a chain during the

The monument at Farley Mount

Napoleonic period; in the vestry at Farley Chamberlayne Church, hung high in the rafters, is a *cresset beacon* which could date from the reign of Edward III, used at Farley Mount at the time of the *Armada* when a signal of fire stretched across the land gave warning of the approach of the Spanish fleet.

Middle section

The large house at the top is *Braishfield Manor*, built as a farm house in 1550 and known then as Pitt House. It was enlarged in 1760 and in this century new wings were added. During the 1920s and 1930s Mrs Maude King, a famous breeder of hackney ponies, and her husband Alfred lived at The Manor. Mrs King was a great benefactress to the village, presenting the school with a recreation ground and regularly entertaining village children at Christmas. In the other corner is the *memorial on Farley Mount* featured also in the King's Somborne panel.

To the lower right is the red brick *parish church of All Saints*, built only in 1855. The bell tower and clock were added in 1902 to commemorate the Coronation of King Edward VII. To the left of the parish church is the *United Reformed Church*, built in 1818 as a Congregational Chapel and enlarged in

1906. It became the United Reformed Church in 1971 on the union of the Congregational Church with the Presbyterians. In the centre of the panel is the *imposing war memorial*.

The *village pond* on the right, with *children* playing on the banks, has since been dredged and relined. The *willow tree* is no longer there, but *children* regularly feed the resident ducks and moorhens. Below the pond is *the school*, built by the Michelmersh School Board in 1876 with a new extension, built in the Victorian style to blend in with the original, called the Elizabeth Sheppard wing in memory of a very popular headteacher. *Children* play netball in the playground. Below and to the left of the United Reformed Church is a *scarecrow*, recalling that Pucknell Farm in the parish was used as 'Scatterbrook Farm' for the television series 'Worzel Gummidge' starring Jon Pertwee.

The public house is the *Newport Inn*.

In the bottom left corner is a remarkable village character *Reginald Guy (Boxer) Old* with his steam tractor *'Boxer's Beauty'*. Boxer's whole life was spent in agriculture. In the days before combine harvesters Boxer and his father Walter went from farm to farm with their threshing tackle: engine; threshing machine, water cart, elevator and caravan. In his later years he went, with Beauty, to many steam rallies. He died in 1980 and his coffin was taken to church on a trailer pulled by Beauty.

Lower border

Representative plant life: *ragged robin, cedar tree* (several grow in the gardens of the larger houses); *cowslip*; *wild orchid*; *bluebell* and *foxgloves*.

Braishfield pond

Romany gypsy caravan

LOCKERLEY

Lockerley, a scattered village with four greens, lies in the valley of the River Dun which joins the Test at Dunbridge. The area would have been known to travellers on the ancient Ridgeway along Dean Hill and Tope Hill five thousand years ago. By 1000 BC there was a settlement at Canefield where Bronze Age pottery was discovered in 1940.

Top border

In the centre is the *Victoria Cross* won on 26th August 1914 (one of the earliest in the War) by Bombardier Fred Luke who lived at Lockerley Green and who served with the 37th Battery Field Artillery at Le Cateau when the battery was overrun by Germans and two guns were lost. Fred and two companions managed to retrieve one of the guns under heavy fire and all three were awarded the V.C; on either side are *trout* found in the River Dun.

Middle section

The design is based on the four village greens. At the top left is *Top Green*, the highest, surrounded by a mixture of *old and modern houses*. In the top centre is *Dean Hill*, while top right is *Holbury* where there is still a mill by the river. Running diagonally across the panel is a stretch of the *railway line* that runs from Salisbury through Romsey to Portsmouth, with a busy station at Dunbridge. On the left, below Top Green, is *Lockerley Post Office*, while the *yellow faced building* on the right is the *village stores*. Both play an important part in the communal life of the village. Below the stores are the man-made *Lockerley Ponds*, created to provide commercial fishing facilities. The *River Dun* runs under the *ancient mill*, now a private residence.

On the right of the river is the *parish church of St John the Evangelist*. For a short time Lockerley had two churches side by side as the present church was consecrated on 16th October 1890 while the ancient church was not demolished until the following year. Stones are set in the ground to denote the exact position of the old church and daffodils mark the lines of the walls. The new church was built by Frederick Dalgety, at a cost of between £6,000 and £7,000, with timber for the pews and the chancel ceiling coming from forests in New Zealand owned by the Dalgety family, squires of Lockerley from Tudor times.

Parish Church of St John, Lockerley

Below the cornfield on the left is the *school* and next to it the *village hall*. After the formation of the Lockerley Hall Estate in the mid 18th century the pressing need for a school in the village was met by the generosity of Frederick Dalgety and another landowner, Sir Francis Goldsmid. The school was opened in 1871 and still meets the needs of local primary school children. The village hall was also given to the village by the Dalgety family after the First World War. The school and hall face on to *Butts Green*, so called because of its links with archery and used for the village fete, various sports and social gatherings.

Critchells' Green is a little off the beaten track and is rather more wild than the others. *Critchells' farm house*, shown at the bottom, is one of the oldest houses in the village, built probably in the 16th century.

Lower border

This shows birds quite common near the river and around the area – *swans*, *moorhens* and *Canada geese*.

Holbury Mill, Lockerley

Awbridge
Sherfield English
Wellow

Awbridge

SHERFIELD ENGLISH

WELLOW

AWBRIDGE, SHERFIELD ENGLISH and WELLOW

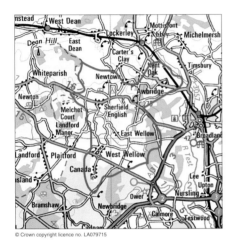

© Crown copyright licence no. LA079715

AWBRIDGE

As an ecclesiastical parish, Awbridge (pronounced Aybridge) is comparatively new, having been carved out of surrounding parishes in the 1870s. The civil parish is even newer having been part of Sherfield English parish until 1984. The name Awbridge derives from Abedric as in the Domesday Book, which by the 12th century had become Abrigg, or 'Abbot's ridge'.

Top border

The school. This was opened as a Board School in 1877 and with all such schools it was attended by pupils of all ages until the early 1950s when, it became a 5-11 years Primary School. The school now serves a wide area, drawing pupils from Sherfield English, Michelmersh, Timsbury, Newtown, Carters Clay and, of course, Awbridge itself, with, currently, 150 pupils on roll. The school recently won a Hampshire Schools' Garden award for the development of a knot garden based on a Tudor design; *All Saints Church*: until the church was built in 1885/86 (of brick and Swanage stone in Gothic style at a cost of £2,800) parishioners had to walk to Michelmersh for Services. The greater part of the cost of All Saints was subscribed

Awbridge School

by the Rev T H Tragett. There is just one bell. An extension was built in 1993.

Middle section

Awbridge is a loosely connected series of hamlets with the main population centred around *Kents Oak* which dominates the panel. This prominent, magnificent, tree is probably several centuries old. The *high ground* in the panel denotes the hilly nature of the parish, with Abbot's Ridge in mind. The *tractor* on the left in the ploughed field symbolises the agricultural nature of the locality while *the golfer*, swinging his club on the right, the Dunwood Manor Golf Course between Awbridge and Sherfield English. The golf course is in Danes Road, a name which recalls the troubled times of the Danish occupation. There is a fort, probably Danish, just outside the parish boundary.

There are several trout lakes in the area but *the lake* in the panel behind Kents Oak is at Awbridge Danes. This was created in the 1920s to provide work for the local unemployed, each man receiving one shilling (5p) a day and a loaf of bread.

The *Friesian cow and calf* on the right of the tree and *the chickens* on the left represent local dairy and egg farming. The rather unusual four-sided *parish notice board* was presented to the newly formed Parish Council in 1984 by the equally newly formed Community Association. Soaring into the sky above the tree is a *hot air balloon* owned by a local enthusiast, Mr Barker. The balloon was a familiar sight, taking off from the golf course.

Lower border

Rhododendrons representing the many banks of shrubs to be seen in the locality; *mushrooms*, from the local mushroom farm, an important employer of part time workers.

Awbridge

Rhododendrons

Sherfield English Church

Dunwood Manor Golf Club

SHERFIELD ENGLISH

Sherfield English is one of the parishes to the west of Romsey and reaches the Wiltshire border. It has many of the characteristics of the New Forest and its flora, with larger and older trees and denser undergrowth than the rest of Test Valley.

It is a small village along the A27, Romsey to Salisbury road with little more than the church, the Hatchet Inn, the village hall, a garage and a few houses to catch the eye of the speeding motorist. Many of its cottages and lonely farms are located down narrow, winding lanes. At the time of the Domesday Book the name was Sirefelle which by the 16th century had become Shervill. The name English derives from the l'Engleys family. It is not known when the family became tenants of the manor but Gilbert l'Engleys held land in the neighbourhood as early as 1254 and Richard l'Engleys is mentioned in 14th century documents.

Top border

Shield of Smith of Ellingham. Bartholomew Smith bought the estate in 1629 from the Tichborne family but continued to lease it to them. The last member of the family to hold it was Henry Lockhard Smith who sold it to Louisa Lady Ashburton in 1903; *shield of the l'Engleys* referred to above; *shield of Ringwood family*. In 1428 the manor was acquired by Thomas Ringwood and was held by the family until 1566.

Middle section

The panel was designed to depict a representative scene in springtime through the hills with the *church* dominating the picture as it does the parish. The church, dedicated to St Leonard, is the third to stand in the village. The first was about a quarter of a mile north of the site of the present church. The second was built in 1858 by the Rev the Hon F Baring but was pulled down in 1902-03 on the grounds that it was unsafe. The present church was given to the village in 1903 by Lady Ashburton in memory of her only child Mary Florence, Marchioness of Northampton, who died in 1902. The tall, spired church built of red brick with stone dressings, with its square tower, flying buttresses and pinnacles, is a local landmark. The interior is rich in detail with art nouveau glass in the windows. The church has an impressive peal of 8 bells. In the bottom left hand corner is part of the *old churchyard and wall*. To its right is the *path to the church* through *daffodil and bluebell woods*, with specimen trees and typical wild flowers in grass and gravel.

Lower border

Hedgerow fruits – *brambles* and *rosehips*.

WELLOW

Wellow was once two parishes separated by the River Blackwater, East Wellow in Hampshire and West Wellow in Wiltshire. In 1895 the county boundary was moved and West Wellow was brought into Hampshire and the two combined to form the parish of Wellow. Its origins go back to at least 825 when King Alfred left 'the toune of Welewe' in his will to his eldest daughter Ethelgifu. In the Domesday Book 'Welue' was held by Agemund who had five 'hides' of about 600 acres there. In 1251 Henry III granted a charter to Wellow to hold an annual fair on the eve of St Margaret's Day, probably in the neighbourhood of St Margaret's Church.

Top border

Shield of the Gurnays. West Wellow, then in Wiltshire, was held by Robert de Gurnay from about 1240. He died in 1269 and the manor passed to his grandson John. In 1296 it was settled under the name of Wellow Gurnay on John de Badenham; the *Parish Council medallion* worn by the Chairman. It was made in 1987 by a local jewellery designer Lionel Pepper, and paid for by public subscription; the *arms of the Berkeley family*.

St Margaret's church, East Wellow

The manor probably came into the possession of Thomas de Berkeley from John de Badenham in 1330. It was held by the family until 1494.

Middle section

The *country scene* at the top of the panel represents the farming activities in the area. The bright yellow *oil seed rape*, which attracted a subsidy, became a popular crop during the 1980s. Prominent on the left is the *Sounding Arch* which carried a carriage driveway over the road below to Embley Park, home of Florence Nightingale's family. As the archway was in a deep cutting noises echoed under the arch, children shouting, horses' hooves and later farm machinery, giving rise to the name. As part of a road widening scheme the arch was demolished. A seat made from some of the stones stands near the site of the old arch. In the past tales were told of ghostly carriages passing over the arch at midnight on New Year or Christmas nights. To the right of the arch are *rhododendron bushes* in Ryedown Lane.

In the bottom left hand corner *New Forest ponies* graze amid gorse and heather on *Canada Common*. There is considerable speculation regarding the origins of the

Canada Common

name. One theory is that the area reminded someone of Canada.

More plausible is the theory that this part of Wellow was being inhabited at the time people were being encouraged to seek their fortunes in Canada. The settlers could claim land on the common by erecting a dwelling of some sort between dawn and dusk and having smoke coming from a chimney by dusk, a system apparently used by settlers in Canada. The name Canada appeared on maps early this century, which discounts yet another theory, that Canadian troops stationed there during the First World War gave it the name. The truth is that no one really knows. *The trees* in the panel are some of the many growing in the parish.

Prominent on the right is the *church of St Margaret of Antioch* in East Wellow. The church was started in the year of Magna Carta and completed in 1216 and is built of flint with stone facings and a tiled roof. The door is full of nail holes where rats and other vermin had been nailed until paid for by the church wardens. Outstanding are the remains of wall paintings discovered under thick coats of whitewash in 1891 and thought to date from 1270. Fixed to one of the chancel beams is an ancient musket, placed there as a warning against the careless use of firearms after the accidental killing of a maidservant by another servant.

The church is visited by people, especially nurses, from all over the world to see the tomb of Florence Nightingale, the famous Crimean nurse known as the 'Lady of the Lamp' and among mementos at the church is a lamp. Florence lived with her family at Embley Park. She died in Park Lane in London and her body was brought back to Wellow to be buried in the family vault. Her *memorial stone* is at the bottom of the panel. It is a plainly designed pyramidal monument with the very simple inscription below a cross: 'F.N. Born 15 May 1820 Died 13 August 1910.' This was strictly in accordance with her wishes. F.N. was how she always signed herself in her later years.

Lower border

Rose hips and *brambles*.

The Florence Nightingale memorial at East Wellow

Romsey
Romsey Extra

ROMSEY and ROMSEY EXTRA

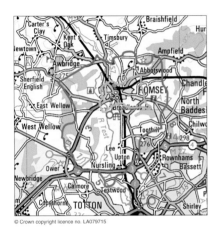

© Crown copyright licence no. LA079715

There is evidence that there was some form of Romano-British settlement in Romsey, which developed on the gravel terrace surrounded by streams and skirted by the River Test to the west of the town. The Old English 'ey' means 'island' or 'raised area in marshland' as here. The element 'Rum' is from a personal name. The river crossing, now called Middlebridge, acted as a focus with roads from Southampton, Salisbury, Stockbridge and Winchester.

It was to the Abbey, however, that Romsey owed its prosperity. It seems there was a religious community by about the eighth century and certainly by the tenth a large community of nuns lived and worshipped on the present Abbey site. In AD 907 King Edward the Elder apparently gave the nuns a great deal of land and encouraged the highest and wealthiest in the land to join the community. King Alfred's grand-daughter, Aethelflaeda, became the first Abbess. The town of Romsey flourished with all the business engendered by the Abbey, with its rich farmlands, its building works, the weekly market and two trade fairs under its patronage each year.

The river Test also contributed to the town's development, attracting mills. At Domesday there were three mills at Romsey and the ready availability of water attracted others – for fulling cloth as well as grinding corn, for making paper, parchment and leather board. The river also led to other industries such as tanning and brewing. The Abbey still stands guardian over the town as it has for a thousand years but many may owe their recognition of Romsey to the glimpses of its streets and buildings seen in the Ruth Rendell 'Inspector Wexford' TV series, filmed in the town.

The parish which surrounds the town of Romsey (or Romsey Infra as it was known) is Romsey Extra.

View over Romsey

Top border

Shields of individuals and families connected with Romsey's history:

1 – *St Aethelflaeda*;

2 – *Pauncefoot*: The family held the manor which bore their name from the start of the 13th century to 1521;

3 – *Ashley family*. The Hon Anthony Evelyn Melbourne Ashley inherited the manor of Romsey Infra from his uncle, Lord Mount Temple of Mount Temple (Co Sligo) in 1888;

4 – *St Barbe* 1605 to 1723: in 1607 King James I stayed at Broadlands as a guest of Edward and Frances St Barbe. He planted a mulberry tree in the grounds and gave Borough status to Romsey Infra. There is a fine monument to the St Barbe family in Romsey Abbey;

5 – *Portman*: The manor of Pauncefoot Hill was bought by Sir Henry Portman in 1588 and it was held by his family until 1680;

6 – the *arms of Romsey*;

7 – *Romsey* 1299 to 1537;

8 – *Palmerston*: The first Lord Palmerston bought Broadlands in 1726 and when the third Lord, the eminent statesman, died, in 1865, it passed to his stepson, William Cowper Temple;

9 – *Fleming*: The family acquired the manor of Romsey Infra in 1679, holding it until 1736;

10 – *Sir William Petty*: He was born in Romsey on 26th May 1623 and from humble beginnings he achieved great wealth and rank, and was a founder member of the Royal Society. Whilst teaching anatomy at Oxford he received the body of a hanged murderess, Anne Green, planning to use it for dissection. But he found that she was still alive, and when she recovered he exhibited the poor wretch. He died in December 1687 and there is a 19th century effigy of him in Romsey Abbey.

11 – the *badge designed by Prince Albert* and presented by Queen Victoria to Florence Nightingale in 1855, recognising her services in the Crimean War.

Middle section

Dominating the panel, as it does the town, is the beautiful and historic *Abbey Church of St Mary and St Aethelflaeda*. A church was first built here in AD 907 by Edward the Elder. The Abbey was developed on Benedictine lines by King Edgar and was sacked by the Danes in 1004. It was rebuilt. There was a second rebuilding in 1120 which took 110

Details of Romsey Abbey

Statue of Lord Palmerston

years to complete. The present church, which dates from that time, is undoubtedly one of the finest Norman buildings in Europe. It has been said: 'It is music in stone'.

The Abbey was badly hit by the Black Death of 1349. Most of the nuns and their servants died and although they struggled back to some sort of normality, it was never the same. Some of the later Abbesses brought the Abbey into disrepute, gaining a bad reputation for laxity, eating, drinking, gossiping and bad language, spending the night in town or staying late in bed!

In 1539 Romsey's monastic community was dissolved. The convent buildings to the south were demolished but the Church was saved, as the townspeople had no other church. The suppressed Abbey was sold to the people of the town in 1544 for £100. In 1994 a programme of concerts, exhibitions and special events marked the 450th anniversary of the preservation of the Abbey.

There is plenty of interest inside the Abbey, including medieval wall paintings, a Saxon rood, 14th century tiles and modern tapestries. Thousands now visit the Abbey to view the grave of Lord Mountbatten, whose home was nearby Broadlands.

Top left is *Broadlands* in its 400 acre park on either side of the Test to the south of the town. Broadlands is actually in the Romsey Extra parish. Its magnificent site near the river is enhanced by the lawns and trees and you can see one of the magnificent *oaks* in the upper left corner. After the dissolution of the monasteries Broadlands passed into the ownership of the St Barbe family and then, in 1736, it was acquired by Henry Temple, the first Lord Palmerston. He enlarged the house and had the grounds laid out by Capability Brown whose son-in-law, Henry Holland, remodelled the interior. The first two Palmerstons, both collectors, enriched the house with works of art. The third Lord Palmerston, who became the Victorian Prime Minister and is remembered for his gunboat diplomacy, was born in Broadlands in 1784 and inherited it in 1801 at the age of 17. His public life kept him away from his Hampshire home for long periods, a source of regret. Later, the estate passed to Colonel Wilfred Ashley, who, on elevation to the peerage, revived the title of Mount Temple, and on his death to his daughter, Edwina, who married Lord Louis Mountbatten, later Earl Mountbatten of Burma. In the 1950s Lady Mountbatten did much to restore the house to its 18th century elegance.

The Queen and Prince Philip spent part of their honeymoon in 1947 at Broadlands as did Prince Charles and Lady Diana Spencer in 1981. In 1979, only months before the murder of Lord Mountbatten by the IRA, the house was opened to the public, his nephew Prince Charles performing the ceremony. Lord Mountbatten's eldest grandson, Lord Romsey, inherited the estate and now lives there.

Behind Broadlands is *Green Hill* with its splendid view of the Abbey, dwarfing the rest of the town, a location much favoured by artists and photographers. To the right is *Saddlers Mill* with the bridge where, in October, salmon can be seen jumping as they migrate upstream for spawning. Special padding and fencing are erected to protect the fish from injury.

Across the Test, in the bottom left hand corner, is the fine statue by Matthew Noble of *Lord Palmerston* which stands in the centre of the square in the town. To the right is the row of *modern houses* overlooking the Abbey Green while between those houses and the Abbey is *King John's House* and the *Tudor Cottage*, situated off Church Street. A popular tradition is that it was used as a hunting lodge by King John in 1210 – five years

before Magna Carta – but there is no evidence. A document of Henry III records that he granted to the Abbess of Romsey Abbey a hunting lodge built by his father, King John, but there is no positive connection with the house in question. Followers of Edward I certainly stayed there in 1306 whilst he was visiting the Abbess and we know it was used as an isolation hospital during the Black Death. During the Civil War the building was used as a billet for soldiers and in 1781 it became Romsey's first workhouse.

Now, after restoration, the complex is open to the public for part of the year and the refurbished Tudor garden was opened to the public during 1995.

In the centre foreground is *Linden House* in The Hundred, which, with many other places in the town, has been used as a location for the Inspector Wexford television series.

Right of the Abbey is *Romsey Town Hall*, purpose-built for the needs of the Corporation in the 1860s on the south side of the Market Place and now occupied by the Romsey Town Council. Lord Palmerston helped finance the project which

Broadlands

also attracted a government grant as it incorporated the County Court. He did not live to see its opening in 1866.

Below the Town Hall is *Strong's Brewery*, established by David Faber, a member of the banking and publishing family. He bought the three largest breweries in the town, all in a poor state, and built up a very successful business under the name of Strongs. Railway travellers were informed, 'You are in the Strong Country', on railside hoardings, and in the town the sign was, 'The heart of the Strong Country'. Strong's became part of Whitbread in the 1960s and the brewing side ceased in 1980. The site has been redeveloped for offices and houses.

The train, centre right, represents the lines from Eastleigh and Southampton which converge on Romsey. Above the train is the *Sounding Arch*, strictly in Wellow parish, which connected two parts of the Embley Estate and here represents the many bridges in Romsey.

The trees in the top right hand corner are at the world famous *Sir Harold Hillier Arboretum* between Ampfield and Braishfield. Hilliers was founded in 1864 by Edwin Hillier who had trained as a plantsman and who bought

a small florist and nursery business in Winchester. The business flourished under his sons and, in due course, his grandson Harold, who, like his father and grandfather, was an avid plant collector. In June 1953, the day after the Coronation, Harold and his wife moved into Jermyns House and the project which was to grow into an internationally known plant collection was begun. Twenty-five years later, in May 1978, Queen Elizabeth the Queen Mother attended the opening of the Arboretum, accepting it on behalf of Hampshire County Council. Sir Harold gave his collection to the County to be held by them in perpetuity as a charitable trust. After his death in 1985, Lady Hillier gave Jermyns House as well to the County Council and the Arboretum and gardens now extend to more than 150 acres of world renown. The Arboretum is open to the public and guided tours take place in all seasons.

Tucked in the bottom right hand corner is the little *church of St Swithun's*, Crampmoor, built in 1858 to serve a rural community as a school-church. Before 1858 services were occasionally held at a Dame School on Halterworth Hill, or, more often, in the 'large room' at the home of Mrs James Feltham of New Pond. 'Squire' Fleming

15th/16th century manor house in Palmerston Street

gave the land for the school on the proviso that church services were held there each Sunday. On weekdays the chancel was shut off by wooden panelling. The teacher's house was entered by a door in the south wall where the lectern now stands. At weekends all evidence of the school was packed away, the room thoroughly scrubbed and the panelling removed to reveal the sanctuary in readiness for Sunday services. After evensong the process was reversed. A new school was built in 1927 in School Road, behind the Hunters Inn.

Over the years many improvements have taken place and St Swithun's, a daughter church of Romsey Abbey, is still a cherished building with a service every Sunday morning.

Among the wildlife to be seen at the bottom of the panel are: *kingfisher, redshank, longtailed tit, mallard, rosebay willowherb* and an *owl*.

Lower border

Marsh marigold; poppy; dog rose; bind weed; meadow cranesbill; harebell.

The Horsefair

Saddler's Mill

North Baddesley
Ampfield
Chilworth

NORTH BADDESLEY   AMPFIELD   CHILWORTH

NORTH BADDESLEY, AMPFIELD and CHILWORTH

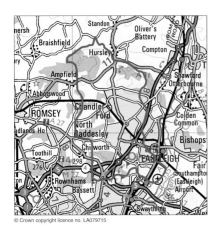

© Crown copyright licence no. LA079715

St John's, North Baddesley

NORTH BADDESLEY

North Baddesley, although still a village, has many of the features of a small town with a parish population exceeding 9000. In 1921 it was fewer than 400 but by the outbreak of war in 1939 it was almost 1000. Its proximity to Southampton and Eastleigh gave rise to considerable pressure for development after the war and large estates of modern houses were built. The most recent of the parish's developments is Valley Park, Chandler's Ford, which straddles the border of Test Valley and Eastleigh Boroughs.

The name Baddesley (Old English 'Baeddes Leah' or 'Baeddi's woodland') marked the northern and southern extremities of the New Forest, South Baddesley being near Lymington.

Top border

In the centre is the *badge of the Parish Council Chairman*. The *shields* include The *Knights of St. John of Jerusalem*. The medieval Knights Hospitallers of St John established their headquarters at Baddesley following the Black Death in the 14th Century. They remained until the Dissolution when they suffered with other religious orders. Other shields are of *Fleming*, Lords of the Manor from 1600; *Chamberlayne*, Lords from 1781; *Mortimer*, held lands from 1086.

Middle section

In the upper centre is the *parish church of St John the Baptist*, reputedly built on the site of a pagan temple. It stands at the highest point of a long narrow ridge running east-west. Parts date from the 14th century, the list of incumbents commencing in 1304. In the chancel is a rare Bible of 1620.

The *chimney* (top left) marks the chemical factory of *Borden (UK) Ltd*, established in 1947. It employs around 300 people and produces a range of goods including adhesives and cling film. Below it is the *Manor House* which was built on the site of the Hospitallers' headquarters, of which the Manor's cellars were probably part. The 16th century building was probably quad-rangular around a well in the kitchen court but the present is mainly 18th century. The *White Cottage* (top right) is one of the few remaining houses of corrugated iron built after World War I. The area was dubbed 'Tin town 'twixt Rownhams and Romsey'.

Below the Manor House is the *Roman Catholic Church*, consecrated in April 1975. Before that, Catholics worshipped at St Joseph's Convent Chapel in Romsey. The first Mass was celebrated by Bishop Derek Warlock. Opposite the church is the *Bede's Lea public house*.

The large white building in the centre foreground is the *headquarters of builders Hall and Tawse*, formerly the factory for Reema prefabricated buildings. Below are a number of plants found in Emer Bog, a 60 acre reserve owned and managed by the Hampshire Wildlife Trust and part of a Site of Special Scientific Interest. The plants are: *willow, water horsetail, water avens, marsh marigold, southern marsh orchid* with a background of *sedges* and *reeds*.

Lower border

Fallow deer; fungi; a *warbler,* a *purple emperor butterfly.*

AMPFIELD

Ampfield derives its name from the spring which rises near the church. The earliest name was 'An felde', 'an' being the Celtic word for a spring.

Top border

The *Gospel Oak with a copy of the Bible underneath.* This ancient tree marked the boundary of the parish with North Baddesley and it was here the annual 'beating the bounds' procession at Rogationtide would halt for a reading of a portion from the Gospels; the *quill and inkpot* represent Richard Morley the 'hedge poet'. His family owned land at 'Anfield' and Richard went to school in Baddesley. He died in 1672 and was buried in Hursley; the *arms of the Heathcote family,* five generations of landowners from 1718; *pottery,* symbolising a traditional village industry. *Bloody Bridge* in Jermyns Lane. The legend says that Cynegils, the first Christian King of Wessex was murdered here in 643 AD, probably by the forces of Edwin, King of Northumbria.

Knapp Wood, Ampfield

Ampfield House

Middle section

At the top is *Ampfield House*, built in 1760 by Joseph White. In 1902 the house and estate were bought by the publishing family of Faber and later acquired by Hillier Nurseries as their headquarters.

To the right of the house is the *Women's Institute hall*. To the left and below is the village *post-office stores* with the *red telephone kiosk*. Since the tapestry was worked the shop has closed.

The thatched, half timbered building in the centre is the *Elizabethan barn* at Hawkstead Farm, reputedly once the headquarters of a gang of smugglers. Below the barn is *Wooley Pond* through which the village boundary with Braishfield passes. In former times local youths would wade through the pond, duck underneath the dividing chain and emerge on the other side to claim a kiss from the waiting girls. At the bottom left is *St Andrews Church* known affectionately as 'the church in the woods'. Ampfield became a parish only in 1841 and St Mark's Day that year saw the dedication of the church on the site chosen by John Keble of Hursley. The ceremony was attended by leading members of the Oxford Group.

To the right of the barn is the 'old' *Potters Heron hotel*, built on the site of the old pottery. A Potter's treadle wheel was known as a 'hern' because of its dipping movement, and 'hern' is an old name for a heron. Nearby, are some of the *clay pits*. Below is one of the oldest houses in Ampfield, '*Mrs Topping's Cottage*'. To the left can be seen the sign of the *White Horse public house*, *Ampfield Primary School* and the *War Memorial*.

At the bottom is *The Straight Mile*, a very attractive stretch of the Romsey-Winchester road; bounded by trees many of which were purchased by local subscriptions to save them from developers. In the bottom right corner is *Thomas the Tank Engine* whose creator, the Rev. W. Awdry, lived in the village as a boy when his father was vicar of St Marks.

Lower border

Badger; *thrush*; *trout* and *dog roses*.

CHILWORTH

The village, referred to as Celeworda at Domesday, is now in two parts, modern Chilworth lying along the tree-lined, straight 'new' stretch of the Southampton to Romsey road, and old Chilworth built around the 'old' road.

Top border

A *Roman soldier*; the *Fleming Coat of Arms*. John Fleming acquired Chilworth Manor in 1827; *Chilworth Manor* which was sold to Southampton University in 1967 and converted into a hall of residence. In 1982 there was further major development with the construction of the prestigious Business and Science and Technology complex; *Tower of the Winds*. This was built in 1854/55 by Henry Lucas, an eccentric artist, sculptor and writer as a residence and studio. It was 100ft long and 60ft high but was demolished in 1955; *brick kiln*, many of the bricks used in modern Southampton were manufactured here.

Middle section

In the upper right corner is the *parish church of St Denys*. Of Norman origin, it had become very dilapidated by the beginning of the 19th century and was rebuilt in 1812 by the Lord of the Manor, Peter Serle, at his own expense. The church is noted for its bells, about 800 years old and probably the oldest in Hampshire. Below the church is the *post-office stores*. Originally built to house the squire's hounds, it became the post office in 1900. To its left, *a rider* can be seen negotiating a jump at the riding school. The tiny *War Memorial* is in the centre and to the right are the *Beehive Cottages* on either side of the drive leading to the Manor. In the bottom left corner is the *Clump Inn* whose name derives from the old earthwork, 301 feet high, on which one of the ancient beacon warnings was located. *The pots* in the foreground represent the Manor Farm Pottery.

Lower border

Deer; *fox*; *rabbits*; *squirrel* and *hedgehog*.

St Denys, Chilworth

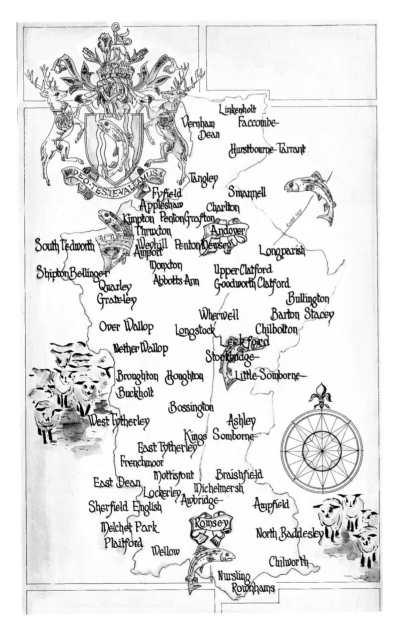

Original design for the Borough map in the Stockbridge panel, painted by Robina Orchard

ACKNOWLEDGEMENTS

Research, Introduction and Tapestry descriptions	Cyril Pigott
Personal overview on execution of Tapestry	Robina Orchard
Editor	Annie Bullen
History Editor	David Allen
Coordinator	Nigel Sacree
Word Processing	Lynn Hellyer and Stephanie Kelly
Design, BAS Printers	Sue Malin

Photographic Credits

Pages 2 and 3	Andover Advertiser
Pages 90, 92b and 105	The School of Army Aviation
Page 130b	Dunwood Manor Golf Club, Awbridge
Tapestry Photographs and page 53	David Facey
Pages 37, 40, 69a, 74b and 115b	Reg Gillam
Page 24b	Lucinda Green
Pages 18b, 22, 23a, 41, 54, 55, 56b, 57, 64,	Gordon Gumn
69b, 73, 83, 86, 91, 92a, 93, 96, 97b, 99a,	
103b, 104b, 111b, 114, 115a and 128	
Page 4	Hampshire Museum Service
Pages 5, 30b, 32, 44, 45b, 46, 65b, 80, 82a	Ed Hendry
85, 130a, 133 and 141b	
Page 129b	Hillier Gardens and Arboretum
Pages 9 and 11	Needlecraft Magazine
Page 63b	Robina Orchard
Page 45a	Mike Otley
Page 74a	John Randall
Front cover and page 98	Nigel Rigden
Pages 84a and 103a	Nigel Sacree
Pages 121b, 125 and 131	Pat Sillence
Pages 17, 18a, 19, 23b, 24a, 25, 28, 29, 30a,	Glenda Sims
39, 48, 49, 56a, 60, 61a, 62, 63a, 65a, 72,	
76, 77, 82b, 84b, 87, 97a, 99b, 102, 104a,	
109, 110, 111a, 116, 117, 120, 121a, 122,	
123, 124, 129a, 132, 136, 137, 138, 139,	
140, 141a, 144, 145, 146 and 147	
Pages 33, 38, 61b and 81	John Walsh

All those who contributed to the production of tapestries, including:

1. VERNHAM DEAN, LINKENHOLT, UPTON, FACCOMBE, HURSTBOURNE TARRANT

Robert Ablett, Stephen Ablett, Brenda Allen, Stephanie Allsopp, Joy Anthony, Budgie Austin, Jean Baker, Nicola Blacker, Paul Blacker, Joanne Brock, Rachael Brock, Jill Brotherton, Ben Brown, Bassy Brown, Nigel Brown, Richard Burden, Sara Burden, Joan Butchart, Susan Carter, Lee Catherine, Nick Cherrington, Abigail Cook, Dora Cooke, Clara Cooper, Magnus Cooper, Lee Cox, Cecilia Curtis, Philip Daw, Jodie Daw, Christine Dawe, Andrew Dewey, Daniel Dines, Julia Dodson, Grace Dowse, Kevin Dyer, Eleanor Fairbrother, Tom Fairbrother, Stella Foster, Ethna Foster-Carter, Angela Freer-Smith, John Freer-Smith, Ewan Gibson, George Gomez, Ian Gomez, Basil Goode, Margaret Goode, Kristie Grant, Sammy Grant, Simon Hales, Zoe Hales, John Hamblin, Sarah Harley, Lowenna Harbottle, Joan Harris , Jennifer Hawke, Catherine Hensman, Margaret Herriott, Muriel Hewitt, Nancy Higginbotham, Simon Hillier, Sylvia Hingley, Isobel Hogbin, Patricia Holland, David Holmes, Florence Holmes, Liz Holmes (Design), Polly Hosier, Samantha Humphries, Sarah Humphries, Turner Hume, Hilary Iveson, Nicola Jarvis, Paul Jarvis, Emma Jenkin, Mary Luton, James Maddox, Dot Matheson, Abigail Maw, Muriel May, Stefan May, Alex Menzies, Valerie Middleton, Peter Middleton, Hannah Mills, Verity Mills, Vernham Mills, Pam Moore, Claire Morgan, Paul Noutch, Delia Page, Gill Palmer, Katherine Pattison, Emma Peart, Julia Peart, Richard Peel, Zoe Pocock, Penny Portman, Agnes Rasser, Dot Raynsford, Catty Riley, Matthew Rose, Simon Rose, Charlotte Ross, Victoria Robinson, Susie Rushbridge, Kelly Ryder, Maureen Sargent, Edward Sclater, Margaret Seward, Natasha Shepherd, Andrew Simmon, Mark Simmon, Gemma Slator, Rob Smith, Renee Smith, Clare Smith, Antoinette Spencer, Darren Squire, Craig Storey, Andrew Strong, Nicola Strong, Wendy Terry, Guy Terry, Mark Terry, June Vining, Jame Wood, Matthew Watkins, Helen Wurzer, Matthew Withycombe, James Withycombe, Beverley Warne, Jonathon Walker, Paul Wallington, Joanne Winson.

2. TANGLEY, WILDHERN, HATHERDEN, THE APPLESHAWS, PENTON

TANGLEY, WILDHERN, HATHERDEN, Jill Donnelly, Brenda Dunning, Kay Griffin (Design), Susan McGregor, Jan Maynard, Eileen Measures, Marie Spencer, Linda Trueman, Anne Vincent, Denise Wilson, Doreen Winstock; *APPLESHAW,* Valerie Baggallay, Monica Bradley, Delsa Brooks, Barbara Chapman, Alec Clarke (Design), Eileen Clarke, Meg Downs, Winnie Howl, Ursula Merrington, Mary Philpotts, Jane Tarrant; *PENTON,* Jackie Atkinson, Helen Burroughs, Norah Bennett, Nancy Bennett, Elizabeth Dampier-Child, Ann Isherwood, Nancy Kerswill, Mary Lawes, Margaret Linforth (Design), Delphine

Maudsley, Rosemary Moody, Launa Nias, Christine Saunders, Peggy Silburn, Mary Stevens, Florrie Tarrant, Joyce Thorn, Dagma Volkers, Mary Wetherall, Dorothy Williams.

3. CHARLTON, KNIGHTS ENHAM, ENHAM ALAMEIN, SMANNELL

CHARLTON, Ann Berry, Dianne Cammack, Margaret Crossley, Jean Dempster, Margery Levy (Design), Iris Lewis, Linda Peck, Linda Marshall, Brenda Mattick (Design), Liz Newman, Stella Snowden, Joy Taylor; *ENHAM ALAMEIN AND KNIGHTS ENHAM,* Jane Borley, Patricia Borley, Nora Bullen, Renee Bulpit, Brenda Mattick (Design), Julia Reilly (Design), Betty Waters; *SMANNELL,* Sue Armitage, Evelyn Bright, Anne Brook (Design), Phyl Brook, Nora Bullen, Renee Bulpit, Mavis Clarke, Jean Dance, Ruth Davies, Joan Figgins, Joan Gilbert, Sarah Gouriet, Virginia Haines, Vyvyan Hartley, Jennie Humphreys, Susan Joseph, David Jardine, Susan Jardine, Jill Loveridge, Brenda Mattick, Peggy Payne, Gilly Radford, Julia Reilly, Freddie Smith, Margaret Smith, Betty Waters, Peggy White, Henrietta Wood, Pupils of Smannell C of E Primary School.

4. ANDOVER

Elizabeth Acres, Patricia Aitken, Elinor Allan, Gladys Allan, Evelyn Allen, Anne Baker, Dorothy Barlow, Jeanne Birks, Felicia Calin, Daphne Channing, Winnie Daly, Violet Dannatt , Carol Grimstone, Elsie Hayward, Cynthia Jewitt, Niel Jewitt, Rosalyn Lockwood, Meg McConnell, Chris Meads (Design), Lynda Newberry, Morag Painter, Linda Peck, Jean Ross, Elizabeth Rowe, Kathy Rowe, Jean Spurgeon.

5. THRUXTON, FYFIELD, KIMPTON

THRUXTON, Susan Buckmaster, Christine Barrett, Nicola Barrett, Elizabeth Butterworth, Elizabeth Cosgrove, Linda Lilley (Design), Adam Lilley, Rachel Lilley, Hugh McPartlan (Design), Margaret Moylen-Jones, Nora Nash, Frankie Richcord; *FYFIELD,* Cheri Baster, Molly Baster, Win Carr, Jenny Forsyth, Azalea Mayhew (Design), Kathleen Pennells, Augusta Rose, Ann Rowe, John Rowe, Sheila Woodwards, Gillian Yarde-Leavett (Design); *KIMPTON,* Debbie Baker, Pam Buchanan, Karla Flambert, Roger Flambert (Design), Stella Flambert, Vicky Flambert, Pat Grinter, Kathleen Henderson, Azalea Mayhew (Design), George McLaughlin, Wendy McLaughlin, Sany Odone, Philip Ray, Arthur Rogers, Mary Rogers , Julie Rustin, Alice Smith, Jill Smith, Jo Turgoose, Gillian Yarde-Leavett (Design).

6. WEYHILL, SHIPTON BELLINGER, TIDWORTH

TIDWORTH, Molly Ayres, Barbara Babman, Mac Baugh, Sybil Baugh, Maureen Dagger, Gladys Fields, Muriel Harris, Eric

ACKNOWLEDGEMENTS

Johnson (Design), Alison Lewis, Sylvia Lewis, Aileen Martin, Barbara Oatley, Edward Otway, Sylvia Pearce, Doris Sweeney, Dan Symonds (Design), Marcia Turnbull, Muriel Vickery, Margaret Wadcock, Joan West, Mary Williams; *SHIPTON BELLINGER*, Sue Ball, Maureen Berry, Freda Bowden, Marie Bryan, Annelise Chamberlain, Robert Cooke (Design), Carole Estlick, John Flowers, Rosemary Flowers, Roz Hanson, Sylvia Hart, Heather Herring, Rozanna Herring (Design), Jean Hinde, Antonia Hiscocks, June Jay, Pam Kearley, Ryan Kearley, Jean Mills, Gwen Phillips, Lynn Phillips, Barbara Pottinger (Design), Ellen Reynolds, Linda Reynolds (Design), Mary Russell, Alison Sperry, Wendy Sperry, Beryl Vickers, Renate Wilson, Val Winfield, Edward Workman, James Workman, Liz Workman, Rebecca Workman; *WEYHILL*, Jean Barrett (Design), Susan Coleman, Marina Colley, Dorothy Elmer.

7. MONXTON, AMPORT, GRATELEY
MONXTON, Douglas Bliss, Bridget Busk, Carol Childs, Pamela Childs, Diana Coldicott, Joan Couper, Judy Crick, Shona Crick, Brenda Gower, Maisie Lock, Winifred Lock, Irene Marver, Meg McConnell (Design), Lucy Munden, Sylvia Potter, Carol Pratt, Heather Pratt, Veronica Rushworth-Lund, Joy Smith; *AMPORT*, Beryl Baglin, Heidi Carre, Sheila Goacher, Maureen Gumn, Catherine Grylls, Marisa Hayhurst, Sheelagh Mathias, Elizabeth Orchard, Robina Orchard (Design), Betty Spurgeon; *GRATELEY*, Maureen Booth, Rhoda Bucknill (Design), Velma Collett (Design), Anne Collier, Lucy Felton, Edna Forsyth, Eileen Jeffries, Anne King, Elizabeth Medley, Heather Popham, Pat Richards, Hilary Seddon, Juanita Sharman, Pattie Tayler, Gwyneth Tierney, Stephanie Wheatley.

8. ABBOTTS ANN, LITTLE ANN
Alan Selby (Design), Jane Simson.

9. GOODWORTH CLATFORD, UPPER CLATFORD, BARTON STACEY
GOODWORTH CLATFORD, Marjorie Eagar, Anne de Nahlik (Design), Claire Russell (Design), Peggy Strange; *UPPER CLATFORD*, Pamela Baker, Peggy Bandy, Pooch Bathurst-Brown, Valerie Combes, Lina Duckworth, Mrs Edwards, Dee Fenton, Mary George, Jennifer Greenwood, Edith Hunt, Rosemary Johnson-Ferguson, Sylvia Kennedy, Judy Marr, Patricia Mason, Geraldine McCaulder (Design), Patricia Simmonds, Rosemary Walker, Barbara Walter; *BARTON STACEY*, Patricia Coleman, Monica Austin, Gillian Beresford, Jenny Briscoe, Hazel Deacon, Wendy Dewey, Barbara Evans, Audrey Freemantle, Moreen Gifford-Hull, Shane Hearn, Julia Hebden, Elver Jackson, Helen James, Susan Lawton, Helen Litton, Julia Mason, Mavis May, Cheryl McCracken, Sally

Merrison, Jean Mills, Margaret Morris, Anna Peebles, Gordon Piper, William Powell, Vera Riggs, Holly Sambell, Jan Sambell (Design), Ann Scoates, Kelly Scoates, Sarah Scoates, June Stacey, Marilyn Stevens, Jean Talbot, Sandy Thornton, Inja Wainwright, Catherine Wilkinson.

10. CHILBOLTON, WHERWELL, LONGPARISH
CHILBOLTON, Mavil Arnold, Frances Batchelor, Michael Batchelor, Lizzie Batchelor, Sue Batchelor (Design), Thomas Batchelor, Ann Blythe, Madeleine Farrand, June Hayman Joyce, Peter Le Breton, Jean Stephens, Jennie Stobart, Edith Vincent, Pupils of Wherwell Primary School, Members of Chilbolton W.I.; *WHERWELL*, Evelyn Violet Hopkins (Design); *LONGPARISH*, Margaret Barber, Sue Elford, Nancy Goodwin, Sarah Harris, Kathleen Hewlett, Jane Jackson, Margaret Johnson, Kathleen North, Anne Russum, Ella Scott, Mary Snow (Design), Dick Snow, Jane Snow, Peggy Snow, Sue Stevens, Rosemary Tennant, Cecil White, Joy White.

11. THE WALLOPS
NETHER WALLOP, June Anderson, Jane Blaxter, Pat Brown, Joyce Blanchard, Mary Butler Stoney, Anne Burkett, Sheila Dickson, Doug Dickson, Sheila Eyre, Christine Fell, Jackie Fenn, Pat Foot, Jane Gardiner, Fiona Gardiner, Jocelyn Gumn, Kit Harper, Catherine Henderson, Antonia Henderson, Camilla Henderson, Venitia Henderson, Rosemary Jepson Turner, Alma Mouland, Sheila Mouland, Susan Osmond, Anthea Russell, Linda Sherwood, Ellen Smith, Jackie Walker, Phyllis Weeks, Margaret Williams (Design); *OVER WALLOP*, Nancy Franks, Jane Gardiner, Marion Gleadow, Catherine Henderson, Antonia Henderson, Camilla Henderson, Venitia Henderson, Mrs Holton, Jeanette Kinch, Jill Lovett, Mary Rayner, Elizabeth Silcock, Mrs Willey, Margaret Williams (Design).

12. BOROUGH MAP WITH STOCKBRIDGE, LONGSTOCK, LECKFORD
STOCKBRIDGE, LONGSTOCK, LECKFORD, Connie Alderman, Margery Andrews, Barbara Belcher, Marina Bulpitt, Penny Burnfield, Lillian Carrey, Gillian Clark, Lucy Clark, Melaine Clark, Edna Clarke, Pamela Clarke, Kay Clayton, Ena Croker, Dorothy Darby, Rose East, Carolyn Evans, Kate Gibbons, Shirley Guard, Monica Harding, Iris Harman, Rosalind Hill, Sue Hofman, Margaret Humber, Jean Johnson, Elfie Kerrison, Mary Lock, Anne Merridale, Mrs Monaghan, Anne Musters, Mabel Nelmes, Joyce Pye Smith, Betty Rawlence (Design), Dorothy Richardson, Mary Saunders, Barbara Shearwood, Dame Nancy Snagge, Margery Stares, Nina VanGalen, Gladys Wearing, Pauline Webster; *TEST VALLEY BOROUGH MAP*, Lucy Felton, Sheelagh Mathias, Robina Orchard (Design).

13. HOUGHTON, BOSSINGTON AND BROUGHTON
HOUGHTON & BOSSINGTON, Georgia Burgess, Sophie Busk, Pat Cannings, Joan Chant, Margaret Carter, Ann Fairey, Terence and Dorothea FitzGibbon (Design), Esme Fellows, Jill Harding, David Howe, Carol Norton, Lyn Snellgrove, Mary Underwood; *BROUGHTON*, Veronica Chubb, Margot Dent, Elsa Drew, Terence and Dorothea FitzGibbon (Design), David Howe, Joyce Monk, Kathleen Palmer, Diana Puckle, Susan Turpin, Susan Joyce.

14. KING'S SOMBORNE, LITTLE SOMBORNE, UP SOMBORNE, ASHLEY
Davina Adams, Barbara Allan, Louise Andrews, Jeremy Aucock, Kristy Aucock, Linda Aucock, Jenny Baker, Vic Baker, Samantha Baker, Theresse Baker, Audrey Baker, Janet Baker, Muriel Bailey, Prue Barlow, Barbara Barnes, Jaqueline Barnes, James Barry, Audrie Bendall (Design), Frank Bendall, Lily Biddlecombe, Movita Bird, Pat Bird, Eddie Black, Barry Blackmore, Lisa Blackmore, Margery Blake, Kate Broadbridge, Barbara Broadbridge, Anthony Brooke-Webb, Joyce Brooke-Webb, Susannah Brooke-Webb, Simon Brooke-Webb, Tim Brooke-Webb, Joan Brown, Win Brown, Anne Burrell, David Burrell, Vera Burt, Philip Burt, Valerie Burton, Dorothy Butcher, Susan Byrne, Robin Cardwell, Rosemary Cardwell, Ann Carr, Jackie Chalcraft, Elsie Chapman, Phyl Chapman, Anne Clay, Ernie Clay, Henry Cole, Bridget Coleman, Penny Coleman, Loretta Collier, Vivien Clowes, Susan Cripps, Charlotte Cripps, Jean Cummings, Joan Dowty, Geoff Drinkwater, Mary Dutnall, Mike Dutnall, Penny Dyke, James Ede, Sarah Ede, Genette Edwards, Rachel Ewence, Nora Evans, Denise Evans, Diana Eubank-Scott, Lynsay Eubank-Scott, Jessica Eubank-Scott, Andrew Flanaghan, Sheila Fletcher, Bill Fletcher, Phyllis Gardner, Natasha Geary, Steven Geary, Angela Gentry, Harriet Gentry, Richard Gentry, Sarah George, Hannah George, Ivy Gibbons, Jessie Grace, Pat Grieveson, Amy Green, Ann Karin Gunnarson, Mollie Haines, Rita Harfield, Julia Hawkswood, Caroline Hervey-Bathurst, Catherine Henderson, Gillian Hilton, Paul Hilton, Alexander Hilton, Katherine Hilton, Olive Hoare, Ralph Hone, Sybil Hone, Ann Marie Hook, Rosemary Horsey, Margaret Howard, Paul Hurst, Sue Jackson, Alex James, Vera Jones, Claire Jones, Chrissie Johnstone, Tamila Johnstone, Berin Johnstone, Sylvia Kay, Sarah Keeley, Delia King, David King, Lesley King, Stephen King, Jane King, Donna Lane, Jean Lane, Dale Lane, Lily Lane, Lilian Light, Connie Machin, Pat Mahoney, Edna Mackenzie, Patricia Mackenzie, Ann Mackenzie, Anna McCay, Nola McIntosh, Judy McPhee, Sarah McPhee, Nick McPhee, Freda Marchant, Richard Martin, Susan Martin, Terence Martin, Jeanne Mills, Pam Monk, Patricia Newell, Hedley Newell, Cathy Newell, Rowland Newell, Angela O'Leary, Archie O'Leary, Emma O'Leary, Lisa O'Leary, Sian O'Leary, Shane O'Leary, Millie Oram, Denise Orange, Ethel

Osborne, Helen Pearson, Janet Pearson, Gordon Pearson, David Pearson, Chris Pearson, Andrew Peel, Amanda Peel, Mary Perry, Irene Pigott, Cyril Pigott, Nigel Potter, Muriel Potter, Richard Potter, William Potter, Jane Purdue, Betty Ray, Eve Read, Mary Rebbeck, Paul Reynolds, Marjorie Richardson, Janice Robbins, Kevin Robbins, Kerry Robbins, Ellen Rumbold, Sharon Rumbold, Mary Rustell, Bill Saltmarsh, Phyllis Saltmarsh, Kate Saunders, Phil Saunders, Ruth Shepard, Daphne Shotton, Pat Sillence, Lorna Simms, Rosa Sims, Mike Simms, Syd Skinner, Pamela Skinner, June Smith, Les Smith, Adam Spurling, Sue Spurling, Robert Spurling, Ian Stewart, Laura Stewart, Arden Stewart, Kevin Stubbs, Jennifer Stubbs, Joanna Stubbs, Benjamin Stubbs, Amy Swatton, Simon Taylor, Audrey Thomas, Sheila Tickner, Kevin Tickner, Margie Till, Claire Tongs, Mary Turner, Simon Turner, John Vanderpump, Lucy Vanderpump, Joan Verrier, Muriel Way, Leslie Way, Caroline Weeks, Sharron Whatley, Pamela Whatley, Andrea Whatley, Iris Whatley, Nicky Witcher, Mike Woodcock, Kenneth Woolfit, Ian Wilson, Sally Wilson, Jeannie Wilson, Robert Wilson, Staff and pupils of King's Somborne Primary School, Hannah Amos, Lynn Amos, Simon Amos, Kieron Andrews, James Aucock, Kirsty Aucock, Dean Baker, Lorna Baker, Michael Baker, Tanya Baker, Claire Baldwin, Jennifer Bamford, Enid Bevan, Aurelie Bevan, Wayne Black, Lisa Blackmore, Helen Bolderstone, Nicola Boyce, Claire Broome, Nicola Bunch, Paul Burrell, Jonathan Cardwell, Thomas Cardwell, Emma Carruthers, Gary Carruthers, Samantha Carruthers, Olive Coates, Amy Coultas, Paul Down, Simon Down, Kevin Downing, Emma Dyke, Caroline Eales, Mark Edwards, Peter Edwards, Mark Evans, Tammy Ewence, Danny Foyle, Natasha Geary, Bernard Grant, Barry Grievson, Wendy Hood, Deborah Howard, Jean Howard, Robert Jackson, Samuel Jackson, Debra Keeley, Geoffrey King, Donna Knights, Charlene Lane, Paul Lane, Max Langton-Lockton, Tabitha Langton-Lockton, Natalie Muggeridge, Wayne Nelmes, David Newell, Sarah Newell, Sian O'Leary, Ashley Oram, David Portsmouth , Jessica Portsmouth, Michael Quick, Emma Rioldi, David Roberts, Victoria Roberts, Thomas Robison, Julie Ross, Debby Sacree, Anita Selman, Lucy Sherred, Emma Snellgrove, Laura Snellgrove, Gary Tickner, Stephen Tickner, Marcus Tongs, Joyce Trueman, Fiona Turner, Richard Verrier, Janice Waterman, Justyn Waterman, Kelly Westbrook, Angela Worgan, Lee Young.

15. MOTTISFONT, NURSLING AND ROWNHAMS, EAST TYTHERLEY
MOTTISFONT, Margery Abraham, Madeleine Aylward, Sylvia Blake, Anne Cameron, Doris Cannons, Barbara Cavanagh, Catherine Cavanagh, Olivia Cavanagh, Susan Clutterbuck, Rachel Fowler, Cythia Fletcher, Canon David Howe, Moira Hulugalle, Edna Mathews, Victoria Muers-Raby, Dolly Newell, Sylvia Pankhurst, Theresa Port, Margaret Spreadbury, Barbara-

Anne Thomas, Joan Thompson, Valda White, Cathy Wood, Gordon Wood (Design); *NURSLING AND ROWNHAMS*, Barbara Dawe, Christopher Kemp, Lin Kemp (Design), Judith Lawry, Bunny Mann, Leslie Mann, Mildred McGroarty; *EAST TYTHERLEY*, Margaret Downe, Ina Redshaw, Pamela Russell, Joyce Sowden, Marjorie West (Design).

16. MICHELMERSH, BRAISHFIELD, LOCKERLEY
MICHELMERSH, Joyce Brown, Celia Cox, Mary Lees, Shirley Morrish (Design), Eileen Newcomb, Vanessa Pink, Shirley Price, Elizabeth Webb, Betty Welch; *BRAISHFIELD*, Joyce Alford, Margaret Batchelor, Barbara Bell, Sarah Boothman, Millie Dunford, Elizabeth Ellison, Evelyn Eustace, Jose Fare, Olive Fuller, Esme Kidd, Marilyn Madigan (Design), Enid Oliver, Ruby Payn, Margery Penton, Patricia Roe, Diana Selka, Elizabeth Sheppard, Magdalen Sleeman, Ms E Stuart-Smith, Jill Van-Rooijen, Freda Vrotsos, Head Master and pupils of Braishfield Primary School, Katie Appleton, Stuart Bakewell, Alexia Bell, Thomas Bird, Charlotte Butterfield, Lucy Butterfield, Stuart Chalder, Beverley Corrigan, Robin Corrigan, Hannah Cross, Daniella Dejonge, Koos Dejonge, Tom Dejonge, Jonathan Forch, Josh Hampton, Andrew Hansom, Jonathan Haysom, Darren Hayter, Ashley Herridge, Biba Herridge, Emily Hobday, Alex Hodgson, Damian Howkins, Lucy Howkins, Fiona Hunt, Guy Hunt, Oliver Johnson, Richard King, Ruth King, Luke Kington, Mark Krey, James Lanham, Nicholas Lawson, Caroline Leach, Ben Leatherdale, Luke Leatherdale, Rowena Lewis, Vicky Lewis, James Light, Joanne Light, Darren Manton, Neil McKay, Morris Miles, Darrel Milsom, Richard Milsom, Colin Morris, Hayley Morris, Rachael Morris, Sarah Musslewhite, Lorraine Norman, Ryan Norman, Michael Passe, Sharron Passe, Lee Payne, Matthew Payne, Ewen Ross, Andrew Scott, Peter Scott, Christopher Spacagna, Jenny Spacagna, Ralph Stevens, David Thomas, Stacey Tiley, Brett Turner, Anna Vrotsos, Sebastian West, Tristan West, Phillip Wildman, Cally Wilkinson, Jenna Wilkinson, Timothy Wordsworth; *LOCKERLEY*, Olwen Allen, Betty Anning, Joyce Bullock, Peter Bullock, Frederick Courtney OBE, Marion Courtney (Design), Jo Earwood, Dolores Ford, Diana McMillan, Margaret Niblett, Mollie Parsons, Isabel Stileman, Margaret Williams.

17. AWBRIDGE, SHERFIELD ENGLISH, WELLOW
AWBRIDGE, Doreen Bethell (Design), Ann Goulden, Pauline Harris, Pam Hillier, Margaret Hutchens, Anne Jones, Rosemary Oakeshott, Joy Skinner, Liz Stringer; *SHERFIELD ENGLISH*, Lilian Biddlecombe, Tessa East, Myra Galton, Margaret George, Ursula Goodyear, Fay Heath (Design), Shirley Lemon, Barbara Sharp, Elisabeth Smith; *WELLOW*, Valerie Braithwaite, Marjorie Dorling (Design), Kathleen Eburn, Maureen Harris, Jean Watkins, Joyce Weberstadt, Psyche Veall.

18. ROMSEY, ROMSEY EXTRA
Mary Akerman, Madeleine Aylward, Marie Bailey, Margaret Barber, Phoebe Bartleet, Iris Bradstock, Jan Brown, Pat Caldwell, Florence Clubley, Sara Credland, Joan Darlingon, Violet Delves, Joyce Downer, Thelma Dowling, Joan Duley, Elizabeth Ford-Smith, Caroline Gardiner, Olive Grant, Dora Grieves, Bib Hale, Doreen Hedger, Joy Hendley, Patti Johnson, Annette Jones (Design), Janet Knowles, Yvonne Matcham, Jan Middleton, Sara Moore, Phyllis Newman, Pam Palmer, R Pennells, Elizabeth Pickard, Stephanie Powell, Nan Ramsden, Betty Salter, Eileen Seaman, Mary Seaman, Carole Smith, Mary Thornton, June Thorpe, Chris Turton, Evelyn Wardingley, Nancy Wells, Grace White, Barbara Whittle.

19. NORTH BADDESLEY, AMPFIELD, CHILWORTH
NORTH BADDESLEY, Clothilde Bulling, Cas Hamilton, Pam Morecraft, Doreen Parker (Design), Geoff Pretty (Design) , Eileen Siers, Doris Stapleford, Lilian Thomason (Design) , Jean Trundle (Design), Phyllis Harris (Design), Pupils of Ampfield C.E.Primary School, Luke Andrews, Simon Andrews, Chloe Anthias, Penelope Anthias, Robert Birkett, Alison Brett, Thomas Burden, Neil Chapman, Matthew Clancy, Paul Day, Christopher Drew, Timothy Evans, Caroline Everden, Roland Fowler, Samantha Garner, Maria Gratton, Alexandra Gray, Jennifer Langridge, Matthew Langridge, Joanna Lawes, Sarah Lawes, Helen Oldham, Alexander Ralph, Simon Rusher, Natasha Scarrott, Carley Stephens, Matthew Storey, Members of Ampfield Women's Institute, Members of Ampfield Parish Council, Members of Ampfield "Get Together Club", Members of St Mark's Craft Group; *CHILWORTH*, Glenna Burdsall, Pat Cameron, Jean Hudson, Joan Mears, Betty Mobbs, Betsy Lester, Shelia Robinson, Frank Stokes (Design), Janet Stokes, Moira O'Malley, Norah Wynne.

Note:	*The details and names of contributors recorded above were provided by representatives of each tapestry group.*

Printed by BAS Printers Ltd, Over Wallop, Stockbridge, Hampshire